The Philosophy of the Vedānta : A Modern Scientific Perspective

Sri Garib Dass Oriental Series No : 179

The Philosophy of the Vedānta : A Modern Scientific Perspective

RADHEY SHYAM KAUSHAL

SRI SATGURU PUBLICATIONS
A Division of :
INDIAN BOOKS CENTRE
DELHI • INDIA

Published by :
SRI SATGURU PUBLICATIONS
Indological & Oriental Publishers,
A Division of :
INDIAN BOOKS CENTRE
40/5, Shakti Nagar,
Delhi-110007.
INDIA

First Edition : Delhi, 1994
ISBN 81-7030-403-2

PRINTED IN INDIA

CONTENTS

Preface

This book is an attempt to look for a possible framework within which the *subjective science of philosophy* can be developed in the spirit of modern science and also independently of the existing philosophies of the world. It would further suggest one more direction for the advancement of the philosophical thinking in the context of modern "scientific" terms. I do not think that the claims made out of this framework of patomic model (see Chaps. 3-7) are fully explored in this book. Some of them still require rethinking, elucidation and possible further applications. As far as the utility of this book is concerned, besides general readers, philosophers, scientists the book may be useful to specialized psychologists and social scientists. The book has its own unique character. The ideas are presented in their most absolute terms; out of which a lot of information on behavioural sciences can be extracted.

I would have never dared to involve myself in such a tedious task of writing the book, but for the circumstances which have forced me to present the great ideas of great saints, though in my own humble style. In fact, I had opportunities to associate with and listen to these saints over a long period of my life. I am grateful to all these saints whose discourses and associations could make me think only this way.

The idea of writing this book particularly arose when some of the papers submitted for publication were rejected by the "wise" referees. I am grateful to them for their constructive criticism in some cases and for the encouragement in the other. Some of the ideas presented in this book arose during the invigilation duties in the examinations where the candidate answering the question paper clearly offers the example of an interacting human being with an inanimate (however with EP-matter cf. Chap. 4) object, while the other arose during travelling in the DTC buses.

I have nowhere made any difference, if at all it exists, between Vedic and Hindu philosophies. In fact, Vedānta (the last part of Vedas, particularly that of Sāma Veda) is the main source of Hindu style of thinking. According to several present day saints and thinkers the word "Hindu" carries much *broader meaning* than thought of by some persons. Instead of going into the history of this term I would just mention a few of its meanings. For example, (i) the persons who lived on the other side (India side) of Sindhu river were called Hindus, (ii) the persons who lived in the region specified by the boundaries of Himalayas and Indu Sāgar (Cape Comarin) were called Hindus i.e. the first letter of the word "Himalaya" combined with the word "Indu," thus constituting the word "Hindu," and finally (iii) those persons "*Himsā se hota hai dukh jinako*" are known as Hindus, meaning thereby that the persons who are hurt by violence are called Hindus. Again the first letter of the word "Himsa" and the first letter of the word "Dukh" form the word "Hindu." Any way none of these definitions of the word "Hindu" gives the feelings of communalism, regionalism or casteism. This is the spirit in which the Vedic and the Hindu philosophies are taken as identical. Often in this book the citations are made from Upaniṣads and Srīmad Bhagavad-Gītā which basically are believed to have their origin in Vedānta.

This book is the first attempt of the author. Any advice nd/or suggestions from the readers towards improving its content are most welcome. Further, the author advances his apology to readers for not citing the work of their liking either from physics or from philosophy; this could very well be due to the ignorance of the author.

Radhey Shyam Kaushal

content are most welcome. Further, the author advances his apology to readers for not giving the work of others, taking either from physics or from philosophy; this could very well be due to the ignorance of the author.

Radhey Shyam Kaushal

Foreword

Since the days of Cartesian Partition, the professional development of modern science which took its firm roots in the eighteenth century, had all along been made on the basis of a conscious distinction between the 'Physique' (objective reality) and the 'Psyche' (subjective perception). In this duality scenario, the role of God, if any, was supposed to be confined only to the latter, while the former was strictly mechanistic and fully determinate in terms of certain natural laws operating in the Contingency plane [1] of Theory *vs* Experiment. This over confidence in the techniques of science was considerably boosted by the startling successes of Newtonian mechanics as well as the allied disciplines of optics and thermodynamics which seemed to leave nothing indeterminate. All this was despite the fact that the founders themselves (Kepler and Newton) had not quite got over the hidden role of God in the formulation of their respective theories. Kepler had been aware of an "implicate order" underlying his mechanistic image of the universe, while Newton had indirectly acknowledged the existence of a similar dimension through the Fifth Rule in his Principia [1] which seemed to transcend the Contingency plane [2].

However all this deterministic dogma suffered a rude shock in the beginning of the present century with the advent of Relativity on the one hand and Quantum Theory on the other, when the philosophical implications of these theories began to unfold themselves. The Western scientific mind, rooted as it was in Cartesian Partition, could not easily reconcile itself to the new Dogma in the form of the Complementarity Principle which amounted to an effective breakdown of the strict cause-and-effect relation for physical phenomena (at the atomic level), and pointed to something beyond the control of human experimentation and experience. That the adjustment was not easy was evidenced by the famous Einstein-Bohr controversy whereby the former envisaged an incomplete status for Quantum Theory to be eventually replaced by a more complete theory of the future, while the latter insisted on an alternative (Copenhagen) interpretation according to which the new paradigm must be regarded as an already effective description of Nature whose refinement is beyond the scope of human endeavour.

What was the lesson from this great episode? The most important one was that it showed up the inherent limitations of even the most exact science whose "objective" pursuits are confined only to the two-dimensional domain of the Contingent Plane [1], "while the vast sea of knowledge lies totally undiscovered before it." But surely this is *not* to deny the existence of other dimensions (of thought), just because they cannot be articulated in precise mathematical terms in parallel with the powerful language of science? Indeed, such dimensions must exist since they provide the inspiration for activities in the contingent plane in the first place, but *cannot be accessed* through objective deductions from the latter. This thematic dimension [1] which governs the very thought process of the scientific worker, is itself a highly *subjective* entity, and is strongly reminiscent of Kepler's Implicate Order and Newton's Fifth Rule, which, in the language of Philosophy-cum-Religion, may be expressed by a single term—GOD (for lack of adequate vocabulary). Of course it is regarded as highly unfashionable within a scientific community to invoke such "irrational" concepts which have no proper scientific basis (never mind the vocabulary limitations of the Contingent Plane!). Nor would one dare to invoke such an all embracing concept in a casual manner like one often invokes an ad-hoc parameter or two to obtain better agreement of theory with data! But this *Subjective* (thematic) dimension exists all the same, and cannot be wished away even by the diehards within the orthodox scientific community. The question of a harmonious marriage between the Physique and the Psyche is of course another matter, despite the setback suffered by the Cartesian Partition after the advent of the Quantum Theory with all the uneasy implications of the Complementarity Principle. At the moment, any meaningful synthesis of the two appears as a distant goal, at least as seen from the platform of conventional science, if for no other reason than the cold fact that the limited intellectual budget of its community simply does not allow for such luxuries at the moment.

This is about as far as the prospects look from the conventional platform of science as the language of the Physique. At the other end of the spectrum lies Philosophy-cum-Religion in which is embedded the language of the Psyche. These two languages, each rooted in its own culture, are so far apart as to remind one of Kipling's disdainful allusion to the Chasm between the East and the West, but the gap now is on a far bigger scale than ever envisaged by Kipling for East *versus* West.

Is there any prospect of this gap ever getting narrowed, let alone bridged? Is it worth even a try? If so, what kind of volunteers can at all undertake such a task which, to say the least, appears quite a thankless exercise? A necessary, but by no means sufficient, qualification for such a band of volunteers is that its members must be thoroughly conversant with the languages of *both*, the former with its mathematical precision, and the latter with its logical strength. Two classical examples of brilliant minds which were not impressed enough by the powers of conventional physics and looked beyond its shores for greater satisfaction are Nobel laureates Eugene Wigner and Brian Josephson. Both are giants among physicists, and this fact ensures that their attitudes and actions would automatically carry great weight within the scientific community. For many years Wigner (now in his last stages) has been involved in the understanding of consciousness from the scientific angle, while Josephson has found great solace in Transcendental Meditation. Again, Fritzof Capra's thoughtful book [3] is a fine example of how an analytical mind trained in the orthodox discipline of high energy physics can perceive dimensions far beyond its narrow contours and discover an intrinsic harmony between the abstract concepts of science and the underlying themes of Eastern religious faiths (Upanishads, Taoism, Zen, and Jainism [2]). Very recently, the famous astrophysicist and Nobel laureate, Subramanian Chandrasekhar, has discovered some remarkable manifestations of universal Beauty through highly suggestive analogies between the patterns of C. Monets' paintings on the one hand, and the mathematical structure of the equations of General Relativity on the other [4].

The Opposite Current, in which people from softer disciplines like humanities venture into the language of science is more rare since it is usually harder for an outsider to impress the practitioners of science with as much effect as when the effort comes from their own ilk. However when such an event does occasionally occur, the effect can be electrifying indeed. A good example is provided by Gary Zukav's book [5] which represents a unique experiment in the interpretation of the fundamental principles of physics in more homely terms which dovetail more easily with the classical religious faiths. Of course Tagore's famous song "Nrityar Tale Tale" (In Tune with the Dance) tells the same thing in a nutshell.

These are but isolated examples of highly analytical minds striving to bridge the formidable gap between the Physique and the Psyche. The impact of such activities is admittedly limited, but it is the principle of the thing that is significant: Compared to a few decades ago when such efforts were confined to occasional essays by scientist-philosophers (like Jeans, Whitehead and Russell), the present-day practitioners of orthodox science seem to be much less inhibited about expressing their thoughts in a forthright manner without fear of being looked down upon by members of their own community. And their numbers, though still small, are increasing steadily. This trend should be considered as an encouraging development for the prospects of an eventually more integrated interaction between the basic principles of science and the classical faiths embodied in Philosophy-cum-Religion, so as to facilitate a holistic approach to the major disciplines of intellectual pursuits.

It is against this general background that Kaushal's interesting book "The Philosophy of the Vedanta: A Modern Scientific Perspective" should be viewed. As the title suggests, the author who is an active worker in theoretical physics has made a valiant attempt to bring together an entire gamut of human experience under one umbrella, and to seek interrelations among them in a highly suggestive fashion. In his own words, "this book is an attempt to look for a possible framework within which the *subjective science of philosophy* can be developed in the spirit of modern science and also independently of the existing philosophies of the world." In this respect, he chooses for detailed exposition the *Vedic philosophy* which (he believes) is the most perfect philosophy in the world. And he defines Religion "as a source of providing certain norms for an ordered lifestyle" which "is bound to be based on a certain philosophy. If this philosophy is realistic, logical and based again on scientific reasonings, then the corresponding religion could be an eternal one." In this way he sees an interconnection between religion and (Vedic) philosophy as a *subjective* reality which may be contrasted to the *objective* reality that is described by conventional science. He then correctly identifies the *human being* as the "describer" of the objective reality as well as the "realizer" of the subjective reality on the lines of the *Vedic philosophy.*

This is strongly reminiscent of the duality that characterizes the measurement process in quantum mechanics within the framework of the Copenhagen Interpretation. The only difference is that the duality scenario is now shifted to the Philosophy versus science level through the catalysis of the human mind. Unfortunately the gap between the practitioners of these two disciplines is large because of the vast difference in the nature and quality of the respective tools and methodology, as already emphasized in the preceding paragraphs. Yet he is able to discern a common underlying thread between these two streams which he seeks to uncover within the laboratory of the human being. In the process he considers a whole gamut of phenomena such as interaction between human beings and the physical world, interaction among human beings, role of consciousness in observations, and so on, all illustrated in terms of a simplified physical model (representing the "human being") for definiteness. For the construction of his model he draws freely from concepts in the Vedic philosophy which he puts in suggestive correspondence with the allied concepts borrowed from atomic physics.

Of course no model of the human being can be realistic enough for a *quantitative* investigation of the inter-relation between Philosophy-cum-Religion and Conventional Science, and Kaushal is no doubt aware of this limitation. Nevertheless a concrete model has offered him a glimpse into a vast array of phenomena in which a human being interacts with his surroundings. Kaushal has made a bold beginning in an entirely new field which is likely to be of considerable interest to philosophers and psychologists looking for fresh approaches in their respective fields. In the process he has posed many interesting questions, culminating in his final query "does the progress in objective sciences lead to truth?" The answer lies only in the future, but somehow the feeling persists that Truth is *asymptotic* in nature, never to be realized in a finite period of time. This is in consonance with the definition of Religion vis-a-vis Science as once given by Alfred North Whitehead [6]: "Religion is the vision of something which stands beyond, behind and within the passing flux of immediate things; something which is real, and yet waiting to be realized; something which is a remote possibility, and yet the greatest of present facts; something that gives meaning to all that passes, and yet eludes apprehension; something whose possession is the final good, and yet is beyond all reach; something which is the ultimate ideal, and the hopeless quest."

Asoke Nath Mitra
INSA Einstein Professor of Physics
at Department of Physics & Astrophysics,
University of Delhi

REFERENCES

1. G. Holton, "Thematic Origins of Scientific Thought," Harvard University Press, 1973.
2. A.N. Mitra, "Duality in Physical Sciences and Beyond," Pramana–J. Phys. **27**, 73 (1986). "Parameters of Physics Perspectives: Principles, Postulates and Prejudices," Physics News **21**, 7 (1990). "Profiles of Scientific Philosophy: Paradigms and Serendipity", Current Science **64**, 162 (1993).
3. F. Capra, "The Tao of Physics," Flamingo, Oxford, 1983.
4. S. Chandrasekhar, "The Series Paintings of Claude Monet and the Landscape of General Relativity," Dedication Address, IUCAA, Pune, Dec. 1992.
5. Gary Zukav, "The Dancing Wu Li Masters," 1984.
6. "Great Essays in Science," Ed. Martin Gardner, Washington Square Press, New York, 1957; pp. 206-218.

Acknowledgements

During the course of writing this book I have been inspired and encouraged by several saints, teachers and colleagues either in visible or in invisible form at different space-time points. Words are not enough to express my gratitude to them. In particular, Guru Ji (Sh. Bindhya Basani Prasad, formerly Professor, D.S. College, Aligarh), Prof. D.N. Bhargava (Head of Sanskrit Dept., Jodhpur Univ.), Prof. A.N. Mitra (Dept. of Physics & Astrophysics, Univ. of Delhi), Prof. G.L. Pandit (Dept. of Philosophy, Univ. of Delhi), and Dr. D. Parashar (ARSD College), are worth mentioning. Several useful discussions with and suggestions from Prof. V.K. Bharadwaj, Prof. S.R. Bhatt and Dr. H.S. Prasad of Philosophy Dept., Univ. of Delhi, are gratefully acknowledged.

I am thankful to Mr. J.S. Patwal for his painstaking task in typing the manuscript, sometimes in extra-hours, Ms. Shraddha for her assistance in different forms, and Mr. Sunil Gupta and others of M/s Indian Books Centre for bringing the book in the present form. Finally, last but not the least important persons to be acknowledged are my wife, Shashi and the younger members of my family, Shraddha, Medha, Mukta and Govind for the degree of patience they have shown.

R.S. Kaushal

October, 1993

[1]

Introduction

1.1 Philosophy and science

In recent years, the subject of philosophy of science has emerged as a separate and an interesting discipline. In fact, it has been noticed that most scientists (particularly physicists), in their later part of active life, either become philosophers or think of philosophizing science. On the other hand, these days, while there is a tendency to give scientific basis to every discipline of knowledge—whether it really belongs to the scientific domain or not, the subject of philosophy seems to be deprived of this kind of foundation. In order to give a scientific basis to the philosophy, the difficulty perhaps remains in identifying a perfect or nearly perfect philosophy out of those available in the world. It is now well known that the Vedic philosophy in its totality can offer a case in point for this purpose. Once the scientific reasoning for a philosophy becomes available, it will not only help in understanding the corresponding philosophy better, but will also make the latter capable of answering several challenging questions, posed normally in science, to their deepest possible extent.

In a way, by bringing philosophy to the level of science we are not doing justice to the former because it has not only accommodated the latter, rather it is also the originator. Apparently, there is no disadvantage in the use of science or scientific analogies to understand philosophy better. As a matter of fact for the purposes of categorizing the philosophies of the world in terms of their merits, there seems to exist a need for a discipline like *science of philosophy* provided the latter is known to all its perfection. No doubt, such a science has to be a subjective one.

1.2 Religion and science

The religion, if defined as a source of providing certain norms for an ordered life-style, is then bound to be based on a certain philosophy. If this philosophy is realistic, logical and based again on scientific reasonings, then the corresponding religion could be an eternal (or a longer-lived) one. This scientific reasoning indeed brings in a visible connection between religion and science. As we know that scientific thoughts are functions of time in terms of their experimental tests, religious thoughts in their absolute terms (i.e. philosophical part) should also be functions of time unless they are already perfect in all respects. Vedic philosophy again offers a case in point for such a perfection.

While science describes one type of (objective) reality of Nature; religion, as defined above, also makes one to realize another type of (subjective) reality of Nature. That is why they have been going on hand-in-hand for centuries. Unfortunately, the describer of the objective reality and the realizer of the subjective reality is the same human being about whom none of the philosophies of the world has said as vividly as the Vedic philosophy. In the absence of a clear picture of the human being itself the boundary-line between religion and science cannot be made clearer. As a result, the gap between the ideas of religious leaders and those of scientists in the world is increasing continuously in spite of the fact that there exists an overlapping region between the two. As a matter of fact none of these realities needs to be ignored from the point of view of having a harmonized and perfect society to live in. In such a situation it becomes desirable not only to study the human being and the Nature separately but also to study their mutual interactions in a *language* which is understandable to both philosophers and scientists. In spite of talking of philosophy of science, scientists have been however, ignoring such a terminology. With a view to obtaining answers to some of the challenging questions such as the problem of quantum measurement in physics and the question of understanding the phenomena of birth and death in biosciences posed by the scientists **(physicists and bioscientists, in particular) these discussions** cannot be postponed indefinitely.

1.3 Human being and its behaviour

The human behaviour basically reflects an overall effect of the accumulated end-products of a large number of processes taking place not only inside the human being but also as a result of its interactions with the surroundings at the same time. Surroundings, in fact, again consist of both living and nonliving physical objects. Thus, even if one understands the individual human being, may be in terms of a model, then for a complete understanding of its behaviour, the knowledge not only of is surroundings but also of its interaction with them is essential. Further, this knowledge has to be of somewhat deeper level if the behaviour of the human being really has to be studied in precise and absolute terms; otherwise the statistical or empirical studies as they have been carried out in social and other allied sciences in recent years, somehow cannot be as accurate as desired. A brief discussion of some of these ideas about the human being and the Nature will be further continued in the next chapter.

As a whole the interaction of the human being either with the living or with the non-living objects turns out to be a complicated one. No doubt, in recent years physical theories have touched upon some of the aspects of this latter-type interaction but that too in a highly restricted sense as will be clear in Chapter 6. In fact, the lack of understanding of these interactions appears to be the main difficulty in bringing the subjective science on par with the objective science. Further, since a society is the collective version of individual human beings, the behaviour of a human being in terms of these basic interactions is again going to be reflected, to some extent, in the characteristics of that society.

Science in general and natural sciences in particular are basically the objective disciplines of knowledge. They rely more on the objective part of the observations (measurements) than their subjective part. On the other hand, these days even social studies, while becoming more and more data based rather than just descriptive disciplines, are designated as sciences. Broadly speaking, the basic difference between these two types of sciences is the degree of empiricism involved in them. Empiricism is another name for the degree of subjectivity associated with a particular discipline. In other words, the laws of natural sciences (mainly those of physics) seem to have roots in philosophy. But they are derived intrinsically from the data. While the data in natural sciences are relatively more objective and are taken under idealized (man-made) conditions, in social sciences they are, however, less objective and more subjective. In fact, the conditions here are not completely idealized (man-made). Consider the latter case. Here the objects on which the data are collected are the beings, human or animal. They not only have a large degree of free-will but also a complicated structure of themselves, in the sense of philosophy. This in fact allows relatively more scope for empiricism (or subjectivity) and a lesser degree of exactness. As a result, the data in social and similar sciences remains more of a statistical nature. In Chapter 4, we shall highlight some of the thrust areas in modern physics, where again the degree of subjectivity is expected to play a dominant role.

1.4 Exotic phenomena

There exists a variety of exotic phenomena in human behaviour and thinking, which appear to be somewhat spurious to a scientific mind and as such there does not exist any explanation for them in scientific terms. On the other hand, while some of these phenomena are experienced by Saints and Yogis in their varied form, others are experienced by common men of different races of the world and at different times. For example, experiences at the time of death, telepathic predictions/communications, description about ghosts or about previous birth and other similar parapsychological experiences, are often heard differently from different persons. Besides this, predictions are also made on the basis of palmistry or astrology about one's behaviour. However, some of these phenomena, particularly the latter-type one, have an empirical or statistical basis and they can be understood to a certain extent in terms of space-time coordinates of the human being at the time of its birth. Obviously, there is no place for any explanation whatsoever of most of these phenomena in terms of the objective sciences. Knowing full-well that there are limitations on the laws of these objective sciences, scientists discard outrightly even the occurrence of these rather supernatural phenomena unless they themselves are involved in them. Even if one accepts the occurrence of these phenomena there is no explanation in terms of the existing laws of science (whether physics or biology). Also, explanation does not exist in science for the different stages of meditation of a Yogi except for an objective analysis of body's physiological changes.

It may be mentioned that an explanation of most of the above stated phenomena needs a subjective-type of science. This subjective science, while expected to rely more on the individual's realizations and experiences rather than on the objective data, however, has to be based on much deeper principles than those of the objective sciences. Moreover, the role of the realizing instrument i.e. the human being in this case, becomes much more vital. In the following chapters, an attempt is made to look for a possible framework in which an explanation of all the above mentioned phenomena can be sought.

Finally, before presenting the arrangement of chapters in the book, a few remarks about the word "analogy" are essential as the spirit of this word will be the basis of discussions in various chapters. Literally, "analogy" means similarity or parallelism. This similarity could be of just a concept, or of a sequence of concepts, or of a description or a model, or of the phenomenon as a whole. Further, these analogies could be well within the same discipline or in different disciplines of knowledge. Any way, the analogies, if found, help a lot not only in the development of ideas but also in their better understanding if these ideas happen to be of abstract-type. In this book while several analogies between the concepts of physics and the human behaviour are frequently mentioned, some of them are elaborated to their maximum extent.

In the next chapter we briefly summarize the existing ideas about the human being and the nature in philosophical terms and, about life and matter in scientific terms. Limitations on the laws of science are also pointed out here. In Chapter 3, we propose a philosophical atom-type model (in brief it is called [1] "patomic" model all throughout) for the human being and discuss the interaction of the human being with the physical world in Chapter 4. As a continuation of these ideas, the role of consciousness in scientific observations is discussed in Chapter 5. In Chapter 6, we try to understand the interaction among human beings within a simplified version of the patomic model, i.e., by introducing the existence of three forms for the human being. Here one can find an explanation for the above mentioned supernatural phenomena. As an application of the patomic model, we present a unified approach to the modelling process in science and religion in Chapter 7 wherein it is established that the scientists are the greatest "idol" worshippers. In Chapter 8, we highlight some of the further applications of the patomic model with reference to physics, scientific epistemology, social sciences, psychology and parapsychology. Finally, some important conclusions drawn from these studies are summarized in Chapter 9. It may be mentioned that all throughout, the Vedānta philosophy has been in the background and often citations are made from various epics such as Upaniṣads and Srīmad Bhagavad-Gītā.

[2]

Human Being and Nature *vis-a-vis* Life and Matter

The behaviour or the functioning of the human beings, as mentioned in the previous chapter, is partly controlled by its surroundings. While surrounding may consist of both living and non-living things, in this chapter, the word "Nature" will be used only for non-living (or inanimate) objects. In fact, human being and nature are complimentary to each other. Since its birth the human being while starts depending upon nature for its survival on the one hand, it is also the human being who is admirer of nature on the other. As a matter of fact it is only the presence of consciousness in the human being which makes it different from the Nature; otherwise both are one and the same. Further, the consciousness, as will be argued in Chaps. 4 and 7, also affects the interaction of the human being with the surrounding inanimate objects. With all the essences of life, the human being itself is a complicated object [2]. On the other hand, in its varied form the Nature also appears to be much more complicated.

Besides their aesthetic description by poets, both human being and Nature have also been talked by scientists and philosophers. No doubt, in recent years, the scientific advancements have immensely enhanced the level of understanding about both of them, but it is still much far from the perfection. Bioscientists while have been able to understand the mechanism and functioning of the human body to a considerable extent, natural scientists have also not left any stone unturned in understanding the Nature. In spite of all this the challenging problems still remain to be resolved at several fronts in both biological and natural sciences. In the next section, we briefly outline the present day understanding about life, matter and their mutual interconnection. Further, in Sect. 2.2, we make a brief survey of the famous mind-brain problem and finally discuss the ideas in sect. 2.3.

2.1. Life and matter

For the purpose of understanding the human being with reference to its surroundings one has to learn about (i) its detailed structure including the role of life or consciousness present in it, and (ii) its interaction not only with the physical (inanimate) world but also with other beings (human or animal). Although the details of such studies will be pursued in the forthcoming chapters, still a few remarks about life, matter and their mutual connection are essential here.

As far as the understanding of consciousness and its role in the objective sciences is concerned, it appears that very little has been achieved on this front. Even the understanding of the mechanisms responsible for birth and death of a human being still remains an open problem in biosciences in spite of now having the test-tube babies. On the other hand, the role of consciousness in the interaction between the human being and the inanimate objects in physical sciences has not yet become clear in spite of a fair degree of understanding of the biggest and the smallest in the universe. In this respect the limitations on the laws of science in general and that of physics, in particular, come in the way. Since the laboratory test of each and every idea in objective science is a prerequisite and any effect of consciousness in absolute terms is going to be a subjective one, this also puts constraints on the objective science. Moreover while consciousness could be of different degree in different situations for the same human being, it is definitely going to be different for different human beings. In these circumstances the results of laboratory-tests pertaining to consciousness cannot be made universal and so are the corrections to the physical laws arising due to the presence of consciousness. To some extent such studies can make sense if the subjective science of the human being or the concerned laws in this science become available. With this motive some of the ideas will be discussed in the forthcoming chapters.

The physical world or the universe surrounding the human being also merits a discussion at this stage in terms of both physics and philosophy. In physics, during all these years, efforts have been directed to look for the ultimate building blocks of the universe (elementary particles) and their mutual interactions within the framework of certain standard physical laws and the laboratory experiments. By and large, celestial and heavenly objects in their present form have been understood rather macroscopically in terms of classical laws. The physical world, at its microscopic level, however, appears to be more complicated and requires a lot more concerted study from the point of view of understanding the basic interactions even among the inanimate objects (like quarks and leptons). In fact, except for electromagnetic, the progress in the understanding of all other interactions (such as strong, weak and gravitational) even today is not very encouraging. Cosmological theories deal mainly with a universe consisting of the presence of both matter (fermions) and radiation (bosons/photons). However, inadequacies of these ideas in physical theories, in recent years, has further led [3] to the concept of dark matter (may be hot or cold) in the universe. It may be mentioned that physicists in the process of searching a theory of everything, have no doubt achieved considerably a lot more on these fronts, nevertheless their understanding of the universe in absolute terms remains highly limited.

In terms of philosophy, the matter in the universe has been described differently in different philosophies of the world. For example, Bhūta of Cārvākas, Prakṛti of Saṁkhya-Yoga, Rūpa of Buddhists, Māyā of Saṁkhya-Vedānta, Pudgala of Jainism are the synonyms of matter. Further, the minimal number and the fundamental nature of aggregates of matter (cosmic elements) have been the points of discussion in different philosophies. For example, Chinese recognize [4] them as five namely, wood, fire, water, earth and metal; Greeks believe [5] in four, namely, earth, water, fire and air. Hindu philosophy while deals [6] with five cosmic elements (*pañca mahābhūtas*) namely, earth, water, fire, air and ether, in Jainism one comes across[7] six, namely, *Jiva, Pudgala, Dharma, Adharma, Ākās* and *Kāla.* In fact, Jainism offers [8] a much involved theory for matter in terms of *Pudgalas.* Recently, the concept of Microvita has been introduced [9] to describe both animate and inanimate matter in the universe. To some extent the role of Pudgalas or of Microvita is similar to that of *Tanamātrās* of Saṁkhya philosophy. Instead of going into any type of controversy regarding the number or the nature of the cosmic elements describing the physical world, in the forthcoming chapters, we shall deal with *pañca mahābhūtās* and tanmātrās of the Hindu philosophy. Here, however, after brief introduction a few remarks about the concepts of *Pudgala* and of Microvita are in order mainly for the sake of completeness:

In Jainism *Pudgala* is the most commonly used entity. The word "Pudgala" can be considered as composed of two words "*Puda + gala*," meaning thereby making and breaking of matter from and into the constituents. In fact, it is believed that this process of "making and breaking" of *pudgalas* is going on in this universe. Also, it is not possible to count even the varieties of *pudgalas*. Starting from earth, water, air, fire, vegetables to insects and other creatures, all are believed to be the *pudgalas*. *Pudgala* can never be a (human) being and the (human) being can never be an inanimate object. There has been existing a relation between the pudgala and the human being ever since the beginning of the universe and as a matter of fact, the latter is the manifestation of pudgalas. Further, Pudgalas in relation to the human being are again defined into eight categories. We avoid such further details here and refer to the concerned literature [8] for this purpose.

On the other hand, the concept of "Microvita" has recently been introduced by P.R. Sarkar and elaborated [9] by his follower, Rudreshanand. According to Rudreshanand, Microvita (plural of "microvitum") are living entities which come within the scope of both physical and psychic expressions. Physically, microvita are subtler than atoms or electrons and in the psychic realm they are subtler than ectoplasm. (Ectoplasm is a subtle substance that composes the objective portion of the mind and note that microvita are believed to be neither electrons nor ectoplasm but are just in between). Microvita appear differently at different levels in the world of perception. For example, "virus" (or "microvitum") which comes within the range of a powerful microscope corresponds to the level of the least subtle category. On the other end, the subtlest category functions directly within the human mind. Further, in the words of Rudreshanand "the crudest type of microvita were instrumental for the emanation of life from the cosmos, by creating a stir of vitality in physical structures and by later causing changes in the evolving physical structures of plants, animals and human beings."

It may be mentioned that while the *Pudgala*-theory offers somewhat different style of describing the universe, the concept of microvita is somewhat more akin to that of *Tanmātrās* in Vedānta philosophy. The difficulty with both these theories is that of the minimal number of the basic entities (i.e. either of *pudgalas* or microvita) necessary for the description of both life and matter in the universe. The Vedānta philosophy, on the other hand, is known for describing the universe (particularly, the interaction between the human being and the physical world of *pañca mahābhūtās*) in terms of five *tanmātrās* only. In Chap.6, we shall arrive at five additional *tanmātrās* for describing the interaction among the human beings.

2.2 Mind-brain problem

The main difference between the Western and the Eastern style of thinking about life and matter is that in the former case the approach is from objective to subjective side (i.e. from outward to inward), whereas in the latter case the stress is from subjective to objective side (i.e. from inward to outward). Somehow the subjective part in the Western philosophy is not that much developed as the objective part. Therefore, the foundation of the Western philosophy remains rather weak. On the other hand, it appears that the Vedānta philosophy not over the centuries but over the epochs has been developed to its maximum perfection except for its description in a language like mathematics. As far as the mind-brain problem (or its other synonyms in more general terms such as mind and body, life and matter or human being and nature) is concerned this can also be looked into from the view point of both Western and Eastern ways of thinking. While the discussion and solution of this problem in an Eastern way is postponed to the forthcoming chapters (cf. Chap. 6), here the Western view of thinking of this problem (i.e. from the point of view of science only) is briefly described.

Mind while sounds as a philosophical entity, the brain (or the human body for that matter), on the other hand, is a completely biological system. The inadequacy in understanding the type of harmony or co-ordination which exists in the functioning of brain (or body) and mind of a human being, is normally known as the mind-brain (body) problem. Till this date a lot has been said in the literature [10-13] on this problem. Western thinkers have no doubt talked about this problem in so many words and styles that not only a common man but also a philosopher or a scientist seems to have lost the faith in such studies. This is mainly because of the lack of a clear picture of the human being from the philosophical point of view. Of course, from the biosciences stand point such a picture is becoming more transparent day-by-day in view of the advancements taking place in these sciences. With a view to obtaining a clue to the solution of this well known problem, present day studies also involve the computers for the purposes of studying the neural network and artificial intelligence. However, not much has been gained on this front except for a better understanding of certain phenomena.

In most of the attempts to solve the problem, the role of consciousness has been invoked without actually defining the origin and the nature of the latter. Popper and Eccles[13] gave an interesting solution of the mind-brain problem. According to them mental properties belong to a separate world (called world 2) and the meaning comes from a still higher world (world 3). Further, they propose a mediator between the brain states of world 1 and the mental states of world 2. Their basic point is that the mind with its characteristic of conscious freedom operates from outside of the physical system of brain. Since there is always a feedback from brain to mind or vice-versa, the discussions of consciousness by Goswami [12] and Sperry [10] end up in what they call "paradoxial causal loop." On the other hand, Srīmad Bhagavad-Gitā, in this regard, clearly emphasizes [14]

Indriāṇi parāṇyāhurindriyebhyaḥ paraṁ manaḥ,
Manasastu parā buddhiryo buddheaḥ paratastu saḥ,

Meaning thereby "the senses are said to be greater than the body; but greater than the senses is the mind. Greater than the mind is the intellect; and what is greater than the intellect is He (the Self)."

It is obvious that what Popper and Eccles and for that matter several other Western thinkers (e.g. Sperry [10], Wigner [15] etc.) have said in recent years, was already existing in the Vedānta philosophy for a long time now and perhaps in a more elaborative form. The only difficulty is to bring them in a proper modern scientific perspective. Some of these ideas will become clear in the next section; others are pursued all throughout this book.

2.3 Discussions

In this chapter, different aspects of the intimate (or rather inseparable) connection between the human being and the Nature are highlighted with a view to arriving at a necessity for designing a model for the human being. Once such a model or the picture of the human being becomes available the role of consciousness in the mind-brain problem, the connection between life and matter or in general the domain of "Nature" can be understood in a better way. While we shall strive for such a model in the next chapter, here it is worth mentioning the ideas of Srīmad Bhagavad-Gītā with regard to the domain of Nature.

In Srīmad Bhagvad-Gītā the domain of "Prakṛti" or Nature is described to be very broad and vital—it continues right up to the inner most existence in the human being i.e. starting from the grossest possible level right up to the subtlest possible level. As a matter of fact in the Gita all actions pertaining to the behaviour of the (human) being are attributed to Prakṛti through the verse [16]

Prakṛte kriyamāṇāni guṇeiaḥ karmāṇi sarvaśaḥ,

Ahaṁkara vimūḍhātma kartāhamiti manyate.

In other words, "all actions are being done by the modes of *Prakṛti* (Primordial matter). The fool, whose mind is deluded by egoism considers himself to be the doer." In the next few verses, the Lord clearly emphasizes the art of living in this world mainly by bringing out the difference between the human being and Nature or between the life and matter at the deepest possible level and in most absolute terms.

actions pertaining to the behaviour of the (human) being are attributed to Prakrti through the verse [16]:

Prakrte kriyamanani gunaih karmani sarvasah,

Ahamkara vimudhatma kartaham iti manyate.

In other words, "all actions are being done by the modes of Prakrti (primordial matter). The fool, whose mind is deluded by egoism considers himself to be the doer." By the above verses, the Lord clearly emphasizes the art of living in this world mainly by bringing out the difference between the human being and Nature or between the life and matter at the deepest possible level and in most absolute terms.

[3]

Patomic Model for the Human Being

Nowadays, while the attempts are being made to establish every discipline of knowledge—no matter whether it belongs to scientific or non—scientific studies-on the scientific reasoning, there is no reason why philosophy should be left untouched from this kind of foundation. In fact, to the present day human mind such an abstract discipline would easily be understandable if the scientific reasonings are available as its basis. Here a philosophical atom-type model of the human being is proposed, which may fulfil this requirement to some extent. Although this model is based on the underlying ideas of the Hindu philosophy but it is very well compatible, conceivable and at par with the philosophies of other races of the world, because the reasoning is somewhat scientific in nature. Furthermore, this model is also expected to throw some light on the domains of physics and philosophy.

The aim of this Chapter is not to touch the open and challenging questions which are generally put before a philosopher, but to provide a tool by which the understanding of the difficult philosophical ideas to a scientific mind could be made easily comprehensible.

In the next section we describe an atom-type model of the human being alongwith the details of its ingredients. At the conceptual level since physics is much closer to philosophy, in Sect. 3.2, we discuss the domains of physics and philosophy within the framework of this model. In Sect. 3.3, we compare the role of the tanmātrās of the Hindu philosophy vis-a-vis that of partons of modern physics. Applications of the model are pointed out in brief in Sect. 3.4. Finally, the ideas are summarized in Sect. 3.5. In the Appendix we make an attempt to write the wavefunction and the Hamiltonian for the human being in order to bring the analogy still closer between the atomic model of physics and that of philosophy.

3.1 Atom-type model of the human being

While going through the studies of the structure of matter in physical sciences one comes across the atomic model. This model, through the inverse square law of forces, not only works at the microscopic level but its validity in the form of the law of gravitation is well known for the motion of heavenly bodies. This fact is rather very well in accordance with "yad piṇde tad brahmāṇde" (whatever is true at micro level, is true at macro level too), the long standing idea of the Hindu philosophy [17]. Furthermore, the validity of this law is also noticed in recent times [18] at the level of elementary particle physics. According to the atomic model of the matter, there is a heavy positively charged mass (called nucleus) localized at the centre in a small spatial region. The light negatively charged particles (called electrons) are revolving around this nucleus in the elliptical paths. The laws of forces as a result of which the electron can stay in any of these orbits (called states) are rather well known; they are the electrostatic force of attraction (given by the inverse square law) and the centrifugal force experienced by the revolving electron. Depending on whether the energy is supplied to or extracted from the atom, the electron performs the transitions to higher or to lower energy states, respectively; otherwise it prefers to stay in the lowest energy state. As we go away from the centre, the spacing between successive energy levels decreases. This fact can be attributed to the nature of the law of forces on the electron.

On the other hand, every human being (not restricted by the boundaries of the caste, colour, creed or country) is considered to have the following essences of life, viz. worldly objects (WO), gross body (B), senses of knowledge and action (SE), mind (M), intellect (I), ego (E) and soul (SO). The existence of all these essences of life is necessary for a human being, no matter how their individual proportions may vary. However, some of them may be absent in the case of animal beings. Before describing the model exactly we first elaborate here on the meaning of various essence of life :

WO = Worldly objects like kith and kin, money, prosperity, lust, pleasure, fame, honour, etc.

B = Body : biological body of a human being.

SE = Senses of knowledge and action : in all there are believed to be ten senses —five senses of knowledge and five senses of action. Senses of action are hands, feet, power of speech, copulatory organ and anus; and the senses of knowledge are ear, eye, skin, tongue and nose, whose corresponding sense objects are sound, form, touch, taste and smell. These five sense objects correspondingly have an intimate connection with the five *mahābhūtās* (Pañca Mahābhūtās), ether, fire, air, water and earth, through the five tanmātrās to which Harrison [19] identifies as the partons of modern physics.

M = Mind : particularly sub-conscious mind.

I = Intellect : the faculty of decision.

E = Ego : This is not the ego in an ordinary sense but a more generalized kind of ego in the form of self-consciousness. In Hindu philosophy the substitute for this word is "*Ahaṁkāra*" and it is also in a generalized sense.

SO = Soul : the inner-most existence, the pure self characterised by consciousness and bliss and which is beyond the concept of space and time.

b = Human being : the equivalent word is "*Jīva*" or the seed of life.

With this elaboration of the essences of life and the ingredients of the model we describe the model as follows :

Consider the human being b (now onward termed as only being) as revolving around the nucleus of the worldly objects WO placed at the centre. The being b can stay in any of the finite number of states specified by (see Fig. 1) B, SE, M, I, E and SO. These states are multiply degenerate and do not have well-defined boundaries as well. In fact,

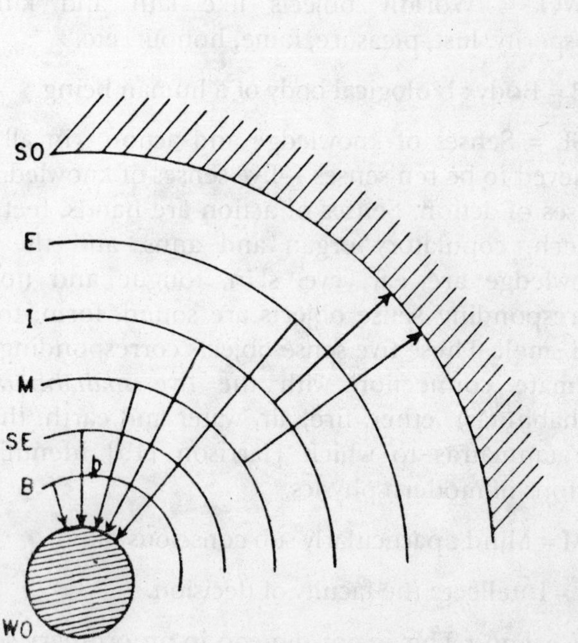

Fig. 1. Philosophical atom-type model of the human being.

every state (except B) may be considered to have a gross and a micro component. The gross component alongwith a fraction of the micro component of each of the states SE, M, I, E, and SO constitutes the state B. In other words, the state B has very complicated and composite structure. At any instant the being b is subjected to experience of two kinds of forces—one is attraction which is towards the centre WO while the other is repulsion which is away from the centre. These two forces of attraction and repulsion on b, in Hindu Philosophy, are known as "*Pravratti*" (attachment to WO, which leads to the outward action) and "*Nivratti*" (detachment from WO, which leads to the inward action), respectively. Of course, the attractive force always dominates as long as the b is in the lower excited states. Note that the state B which is very close to the centre WO, is the ground state of b.

Thus being b can perform the transitions. The downward transitions (towards WO) from any of the states (except SO) are more likely and favourable than the upward transitions (towards SO). Generally, the upward transitions to the state SO are possible only from the states M and I, and that too after overcoming the subtle microcomponent of E. As we go from the state B to the state SO both the level-spacing and the level-width increase in such a way that in the region of SO onward there is all continuum (the shaded area of the figure). Furthermore, the *pervading* property also increases as we go from the state B to the state SO. The importance of the space-time concept is maximum at the level of B and decreases to zero at the level of SO. Even at the level of M it has a negligible importance. In other words, there are no space-time boundaries at the level of SO. For the reasons given in Sect. 3.5 we shall call this model as "patomic" model.

Having described this atom-type model of the human being, next we bring out the domains of physics and philosophy in the light of this model.

3.2 Domains of physics and philosophy

In Hindu philosophy nature is described as consisting of two modes [20], one is lower (insentient) nature while the other is higher (sentient) nature, viz.,

Bhūmirāpo analo vāyuḥ khaṁ mano buddhireva ca
Ahaṁkāra itīyam me bhinnā prakṛtirastadhā.

In addition to the five *mahābhūtās*—earth, water, fire, air and ether—the mind, the intellect and also the ego constitute the eight-fold insentient mode of nature [21]. As far as the search for the laws of natural sciences is concerned it does not go beyond the domain of these eight constituents of nature. However the classification and the understanding of all these constituents alongwith other essences of life, require the mind and the intellect as to play a dual role.

In other words, in traditional philosophy there exists a much wider spectrum of the human being; it starts with the WO and B level and after carrying through the SE, M, I and E, it continues up to the level of SO. For the purposes of studying the interaction of these essences of life with WO and also for the sake of classification of the details of these essences, the human being again offers the mind and the intellect as the instruments. Thus, if one ignores that part of philosophy which can only be realized by Self but can not be expressed by any means—what to say of words—then the role played by the mind and the intellect is rather two-fold–as an object of study and also the subject. Moreover, science can only explain the genesis of life, while for a description of life one has to look into philosophy.

In this way philosophy leads us far ahead of the domain of science, however it does have—may be in small proportion—an overlap region with science. This overlapping region of physics and philosophy (which is termed as "scientific epistemology" due to Eddington [22])

is expected to have many ideas in common and mostly analogous. There are many examples of such analogies [23] including even the above atom-type model. In fact, the analogy noticed by Harrison [19] between the confined behaviour of partons and that of *tanmātrās* also comes under this category.

According to Eddington [24], "the astronomer observes stars; the epistemologist observes astronomer." In other words, a physicist bothers himself only about the quantity and content of the knowledge of the universe whereas the epistemologist has also to worry about the quality and the nature of the knowledge itself. Thus, though the foundations of the laws of physics, no doubt, have to be based on somewhat deeper philosophical interpretation, the degree of depth should be decided in view of the model discussed earlier in Sect. 3.1.

Although, generally we do talk about the limitations on the laws of science but somehow, to some extent, one finds himself incapable of thinking of or believing in the region which is beyond philosophy. In view of the limitations of mind and intellect of a being, the philosophy may also have limitations. In philosophy, mind and intellect not only have to play a dual role but also make an attempt to go even beyond, delving up to the level of soul. The latter is a subject of realization only and hence expressible and understandable by taking recourse to examples and analogies. This is meant by the *Kathopanisad* when it says that reasoning is not capable of understanding the higher plans of spirit—"naisa tarken matir āpeneya" (Kathopanisad 1.2.9).

3.3 Partons of physics and tanmatras of Hindu philosophy

With a view to exploring further substructure of nuclear particles the concept of partons (quarks) was introduced [25] in modern physics about two-and-a-half decades ago. Gaisser and Gaisser [26] later pointed out that the idea of confined quarks or partons as constituents of elementary particles was already present in the Greek atomic theory, particularly in the theory given by Epicurus (341-270 B.C.). Harrison [19], while describing two other atomic systems of antiquity (including the Hindu philosophy), has identified these partons with five *tanmātrās.* He argues that since *tanmātrās are* confined in the sense of being observables and so is the case with partons; therefore, the partons are *tanmātrās as* described in Hindu philosophy. In spite of the consistent reasoning given by Harrison, this identification, in our opinion, is not completely convincing. However, within the framework of the present model it should be taken as a case of certain *analogy.* It is possible to cite several reasons in support of this statement; some of them are as follows:

(i) The laws of physics, which are supposed to be obeyed by partons, may not be applicable as such to the *tanmātrās,* because these laws have their own limitations. In fact, in the domain to which these *tanmātrās* belong (cf. the levels SE and M), precise laws, as in physics, are not known nor are they required in this self-consistent description; (ii) The concept of *tanmātrās* is rather subjective while that of the partons is objective. In other words, the concept of partons (or for that matter any substructure of partons talked about in recent [27] years) is supposed to explain the structure of matter whereas that of *tanmātrās* is not only required to describe the structure of matter but also to describe the interaction of the being b with the matter. As a matter of fact, all physical laws work well in the absence of the will-power and that of the concept of the living being, i.e., they are valid only for inanimate objects; and (iii) had this identification been correct, then all the efforts made in search of quarks should be stopped, which is not the case.

Though the arguments given by Harrison are appealing, they are so condensed that a student of science finds it generally hard to understand them. The purpose of the present chapter is not to advocate an ontology of atomic systems adopted in antiquity by different races, but to provide a tool which may help in understanding the so-called difficult philosophical ideas.

3.4 Applications of the model

By using the philosophical atomic model the interaction of an individual with the world can be studied. In fact, the way in which an individual being interacts with the worldly objects WO, very much depends on its frequency, whether the frequency corresponds to E level or to B level or lies in between. A man of perfection (whose frequency lies in the soul region, SO, and who, in different races, is variously known as supreme power, God, prophet, saint, yogi and so on) and a man who is totally involved in the worldly objects (whose frequency lies in B or at the most in SE region) are two extreme cases available in this world.

Though the downward transitions are always possible from any of the states, the upward transitions are not easily favourable if the being is in the lower excited states, particularly from B or SE states. It should be noted that at any stage the being b is not allowed to leave the force field created by WO. This is, however, possible if the being b is in the continuum, i.e. in the language of Hindu philosophy only after attaining the state of salvation. Moreover, barring a few exceptions, most of the beings in this world do not cross the state E.

After making these general remarks we would like to mention that the behaviour of an individual being, having the frequency corresponding to either of the states B, SE, M, I, or E has been described in different ways in different creeds. We restrict ourselves from going into these details here.

Apart from the fact that this model provides a clearer understanding of the abstract philosophical ideas and helps in classifying the human beings, large number of applications of this model in behavioural sciences, such as social sciences, can be noticed. For example, the degree of compatibility of any two beings in the same state can be realized. This degree would, however, reduce if these two beings are in the nearby different states. Furthermore, even if they are in different states they would have at least the gross component of each state in common. As a result they may still co-exist. Similarly the behaviour of three or more beings can be manifested through this model. We postpone some of these details to Chapter 6.

The model can also be used in understanding the behaviour of animal beings. The only difference would be that in animal beings the states I and E are completely absent while a part of each of the states M and SE is also sometimes absent. However, a gross component of E already exists through B level in the animal beings.

Though the model described above seems to be designed on the basis of scientific reasoning and the observed empirical facts, the essences with which it deals do not lie any more in the domain of science (except the nucleus WO and the states B and SE). They are much beyond the domain of science. As mentioned earlier, scientific laws have their own limitations. Their validity can be questioned at any stage whenever the concept of the being and the will power is introduced.

Like the atomic model of physical science the force laws are not known for this philosophical model. Moreover, the mass-like character of the being b (as we have for the electron) cannot be assigned. Therefore, in the absence of such inputs the analogy with the atomic model remains incomplete and the more exact predictions about the being cannot be expected on the basis of this model. Now the question is : can we think of a law of force for the type of being under consideration ? Or can we assign some mass-like character to the being? Though these questions come under the category of open questions to a philosopher (which we want to avoid here), the answer is that we cannot. Because if it becomes possible then the science will become perfect in its own right and there would be nothing more to be learnt further. In spite of all this we make an attempt to write the wavefunction and the Hamiltonian for the human being in the Appendix.

Here we have refrained from going into the finer details of various states B, SE, M, I, E and SO. Indeed the detailed study of each of these states leads to various modern disciplines of knowledge. Such a detailed study of these states with reference to their multiple degeneracy and to the laws of physics, along with other implications of the model will be reported in the latter chapters.

3.5 Discussion and summary

Using the essences of life as ingredients, a philosophical atom-type model of the human being, which helps in understanding some of the abstract philosophical ideas, is proposed. The applications of the model with reference to the behavioural sciences are pointed out. The model also throws some light on the identification of partons with the *tanmātrās* described in Hindu philosophy.

The philosophical atomic model of the human being described in this chapter will henceforth be termed as "*patomic*" model in brief. While the first letter 'p' of the word philosophical is combined with the word "atomic" to make the word "*patomic*," the dictionary meaning of this latter word can be derived from the word "patois" meaning thereby "differing materially from the literary language" which, in fact, speaks of the correct spirit of the model proposed here.

It may be mentioned that the patomic model described in this chapter, in spite of all its shortcomings, is going to form a basis for the discussions in almost all the subsequent chapters. In fact, the interaction of the human being with the physical world and also with the other human beings will be analysed within the framework of this model. Further, a unified thinking of both religion and science also becomes possible within this framework.

Appendix A : Mathematical Preliminaries

With a view to bringing the patomic model closer to the physical theories, we make an attempt here to write down the wave function and the Hamiltonian for the being b within the framework of this model. Though it is meaningless to talk of such quantities for a human being in a realistic sense, however, for the sake of any quantitative applications of the model these analogous quantities can be defined under some simplifying assumptions.

Let the state of the being b be characterized by Γ which, in general, is a function of a vector V, defined in an abstract vector space, of which five quantities, namely, β, s, m, i and e are the components and correspond to the substates B, SE, M, I and E. Γ also depends on the parameter, μ, responsible for the degree of meditation and it requires a special treatment just as time in the physical theories. Thus,

$$\Gamma \equiv \Gamma(\beta, s, m, i, e. \mu). \qquad (A.1)$$

Note that no quantity is attached corresponding to the substate SO as it offers the background for the existence of all other substates. It is rather a superstate which not only accommodates all the rest but once it starts dominating then b is liberated from all others. Of course, a part of its effect is contained in μ. Further note that m and μ have much in common but they need to be different. Also, β, s, m, i and e have an implicit dependence on μ.

At any stage, the total energy (i.e. the Hamiltonian in analogy with the physical theories) of the being b (as long as it is not liberated) is the sum of inward and outward parts i.e.

$$H = H_{outward} + H_{inward} \qquad (A.2)$$

Here $H_{outward}$ (henceforth H_o) and H_{inward} (henceforth H_i) respectively play the roles of kinetic and potential energies. Further, H_o is a function of $\bar{\beta}$, $\bar{s}$, $\bar{m}$, $\bar{i}$, and $\bar{e}$, the canonical conjugates of β, s, m, i and e, respectively and H_i is a function of $\bar{\beta}$, $\bar{s}$, $\bar{m}$, i and e. In fact, β, s, m, $\bar{i}$, and $\bar{e}$ are the canonical conjugate quantities defined for the same being b after it is placed in the field of *pañca mahābhūtās*. Again note that both H_o and H_i are the functions of μ and the role of μ is more important for H_i as compared to that for H_o. As a matter of fact H_i directly depends on μ whereas H_o might depend inversely on it. Similarly, H_o strongly depends on $\bar{\beta}$ and $\bar{s}$ and mildly on $\bar{m}$, $\bar{i}$, and $\bar{e}$ whereas the situation is just the reverse for H_i i.e. H_i strongly depends on m, i, e and mildly on β, s. As far as the boundary-line between H_o and H_i is concerned, it is not as sharp as in physical science. It is only the dependence on the above quantities which allows us to write them separately. Clearly, the presence of *mahābhūtās* not only activates the being but also creates some sort of dynamism in the essences of life.

To extend the analogy further one can assume Γ to be the eigenfunction of H and write the eigenvalue equation as

$$H\,\Gamma = \lambda\,\Gamma, \qquad (A.\,3)$$

where λ is the eigenvalue. As in physics, if H is hermitian then λ is real. Net effect of operating H on Γ is to bring out some constructive (real) output. If one neglects the mutual correlations among the substates B, SE, M, I and E (which is rather impossible) then one can write Γ as the direct product of the corresponding wavefunctions of the substates, viz.,

$$\Gamma(\beta, s, m, i, e; \mu) = B(\beta)\, S(s)\, M(m)\, I(i)\, \varepsilon(e)\, m(\mu), \quad (A.4)$$

otherwise in actual case one should use the coherent superposition

$$\Gamma(\beta, s, i, m, e; \mu) = \sum_{n_i=1}^{\infty} a_{n_1 n_2 n_3 n_4 n_5}\; B_{n_1}(\beta)\, S_{n_2}(s) \cdot M_{n_3}(m)\, I_{n_4}(i)\, \varepsilon_{n_5}(e)\, M(\mu) \quad (i=1, 5) \quad (A.5)$$

Alternatively, one can express Γ in terms of a complete set of orthogonal functions r_n as

$$\Gamma = \Sigma_{n'}\, a_{n'}\, r_{n'}$$

and finally obtain the eigenvalue corresponding to a particular substate. There seems to be a possibility to predict or to study the behaviour (in whatever imprecise form it may be) of the human being using the above prescription.

[4]

Interaction Between Human Being and Physical World

In recent years, attempts have been made to find an answer to the mind-brain (body) problem [12]. But attempts have also been made to study and analyse [28] the neural networks with a view to generating the artificial intelligence. To what extent have such attempts been successful? What could be the ultimate (possible) limitations of such studies? These are the open questions in philosophy. Again one has to understand the degree of subjectivity involved in these analyses.

These days there have also been attacks from several directions [29] on the foundations of a long-standing, time-tested theory of quantum mechanics. The problems of quantum measurement and accordingly the collapse of the wavefunction in terms of the superposition principle are once again raised after sixty years or so. In this connection while the subject-object division of the world is not properly defined, human consciousness is also brought back in [30] more often as a piece-meal solution to the mind-brain problem. The idea of compactification of higher and additional dimensions to a limited finite number has already been prevailing [31] in the Kaluza-Klein type supergravity theories of physics. In fact, the consciousness in its pluralism is another name for subjectivity.

In order to understand the degree of subjectivity or objectivity in framing a law or in analysing the data taken in sciences, one has to understand the ultimate measuring instrument. One has to understand the human being and his/her interaction with the external world. In Chapter 3, we have proposed the patomic model for the human being which is essentially based on the Hindu philosophy. With a view to finding an explanation and also for the purpose of having a better understanding of several newly posed problems in the domain of scientific epistemology we investigate in this chapter the interaction of the human being (as described by this patomic model) with a material particle.

In the next section, we elaborate the meaning of some terms like subjectivity and objectivity, absolute and relative consciousness within the framework of patomic model. Then, we discuss the interaction of the being b with *pañca mahābhūtās* in Sect. 4.2. In Sect. 4.3, we introduce the concept of physical and nonphysical (epiphysical) matter. While we discuss some of these ideas in Sect. 4.4, a detailed discussion of the rest is postponed to the end of Chap. 5.

4.1 Subjectivity and objectivity

Although it is not difficult to understand the idea of subjectivity and objectivity within the framework of patomic model yet a few remarks are in order. While the subjectivity means something "inward" and the objectivity means something "outward" with respect to the human (or animal) essences of life, an analysis of or a search for the ultimate Subject (doer or seer or experiencer) has been one of the important subjects of study in Hindu philosophy. For example [32],

rūpaṁ dṛaśyaṁ locanaṁ dṛak tadṛaśya draṣtmānasaṁ,
dṛaśya vṛattāyaḥ sāksī drageva nā tu draśyate.

In other words, eyes are the observers of worldly objects like shape and size [33], mind on one hand is the observer of eyes, it is a certain mode of intellect on the other; ultimate soul is the observer of intellect and there is no one to observe soul. Thus the subjectivity—an inward characteristic—and in the language of Goswami [12], consciousness has a varying degree not only to an individual but also to different individuals.

As a matter of fact, the same set of wordly objects (or the data in sciences) can have, in general, several interpretations subject to varying degree of subjectivity. However, within the framework of laws (framed for a particular discipline), set—up ultimately at the level of intellect, such an arbitrariness is restricted. In view of this type of arbitrariness only, several theories in science have been discarded in the past and some are on their way for a similar treatment even today.

In the same way as we have understood the varying nature of subjectivity, absolute and relative consciousness can be explained. No doubt, the absolute consciousness is realized only at the level of soul, but the relative consciousness can have a pluralistic character in the same spirit as the subjectivity. In other words, while absolute consciousness is the characteristic of and originates from soul, its reflections from intellect, mind and, to some extent, from senses of knowledge and action lead to relative consciousness. The micro-component [2] of ego remains in the background of these processes of reflections from different levels. In fact, in order to find an explanation either for Schrodinger cat paradox or for Wigner's friend paradox, the idea of consciousness is incorporated recently in the founding principles of quantum mechanics. We shall return to these ideas latter in Chap. 5.

4.2 Interaction of the being with the pañca mahābhūtās

When the human being (b) (as an entity consisting [2] of soul (SO), ego (E), intellect (I), mind (M), senses of knowledge and action (SE), and biological body (B)) is left in this universe (as consisting of a domain of *pañca mahābhutās,* namely earth (E_a), water (W), fire (F), air (A) and ether (E_t)) a natural interaction of highly composite nature is bound to come into existence (see Fig. (2)). Schematically, the gross and subtle character of these mahābhūtās is shown in Fig. (2b). Further note that the gross property of these *mahābhūtās* while decreases, the subtle property increases as one proceeds from E_a to E_t. The via media of this natural interaction are the five SE's namely nose, tongue, eyes, ears and skin with corresponding sense objects as smell, taste, shape or size (geometry), sound, and touch, respectively. In fact, each *mahābhūta* is responsible for providing with one of these sense objects i.e. earth for smell, water for taste in the form of juice, fire for geometry in the form of light, air for sound in the form of words and ether for touch in the form of sensation.

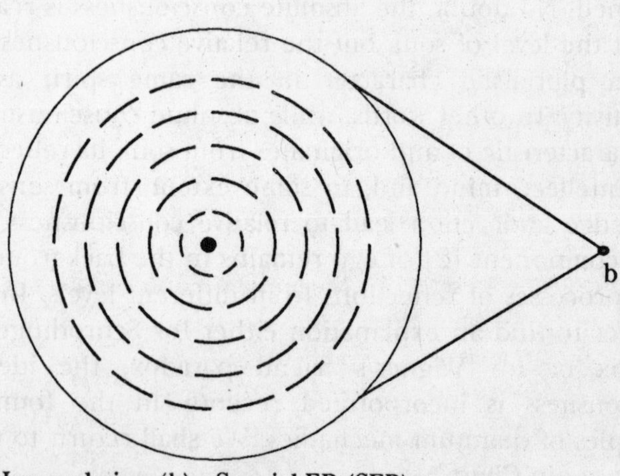

Human being (b) : Special EP (SEP)-matter

(a)

Fig. 2. Human being and pañca mahābhūtās

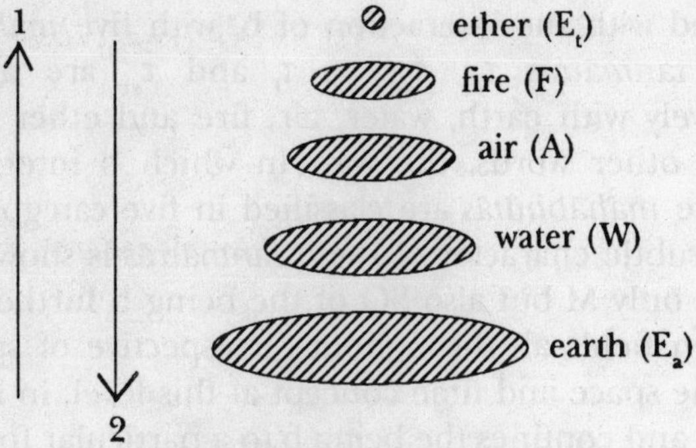

Pañca mahābhūtās : P-Matter
↑subtle property increases
↓gross property increases
(b)

In order to reveal the manifestation of pañca mahābhūtās there is a built-in rule obeyed by the *mahābhūtās*, namely, *Pañcī-karan*-rule [34]. According to this rule, each mahābhūta, as realized by the being b, consists of 50% of its own and 12.5% of each of the remaining four. For example, the earth, as we perceive it, is not the abstract earth, E_a, but it consists of 50% of the abstract (physical) E_a and 12.5% of each of water, fire, air, and ether. In other words, the abstract form of each of these mahābhūtās is dressed up with the interaction it has with the remaining four, of course, in equal proportions. Besides these fractions, each of these *mahābhūtās* is kept again in the fields of SO and M of the being b. We shall return to this point latter. As far as the laws (or in general the studies) of sciences are concerned they confine themselves to the abstract part of these mahābhūtās.

Now the question arises as to how these mahābhūtās interact with the being b ? As mentioned in Chap. 3, Field quanta responsible for this interaction are identified as "*tanmātrās*" in Hindu philosophy. There are five tanmātrās associated with the interaction of b, with five *mahābhūtās*, namely *tanmātrās* τ_{ea}, τ_{w}, τ_{a}, τ_{f} and τ_{et} are associated respectively with earth, water, air, fire and ether (see Fig. (3)). In other words, the ways in which b interacts with these five *mahābhūtās* are classified in five categories. The relative subtle character of these *tanmātrās* is shown in Fig. (3). Not only M but also SO of the being b further extend their own fields all throughout—irrespective of space and time. The space and time concept at this level, in fact, only localizes and confines the being b to a particular form; who, otherwise is spread all over in terms of the fields of M and of SO. It may be mentioned that the field of SO is more subtle than that of M.

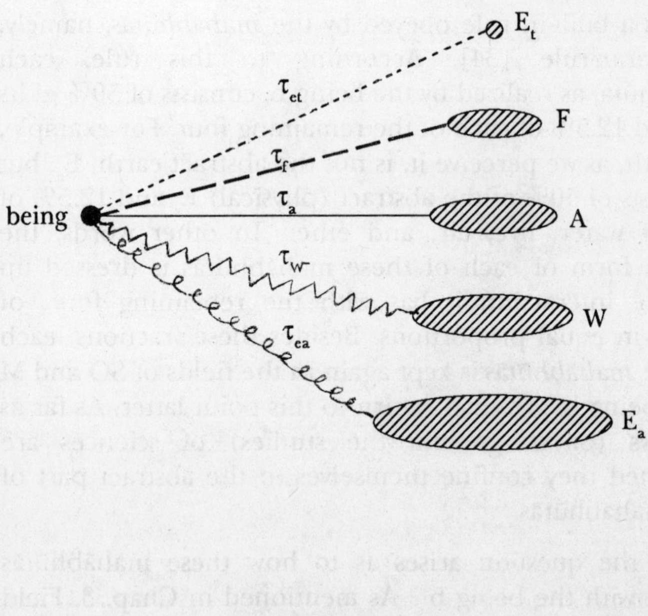

Fig. 3. SEP-P interaction

As far as the fields associated with the four fundamental interactions in physics, namely, gravitational, weak, electromagnetic and strong, are concerned [35] none of them is as subtle as the field of M or of SO. The fields of SO and M are beyond the concept of space and time, and hence also beyond the domain of physical theories or measuring instruments. They are the finest possible, all-pervading, omnipresent fields and offer a background for the physical fields, particularly when the being b is present. It is worth mentioning that while the field of M is of immediate concern from the point of view of accounting for in some of the physical theories (say e.g. in quantum measurements or in relativity theories), the field of SO is of interest to Yogis, saints, and peace seekers or meditators in general.

It is true that the Michelson-Morley experiment could not establish the existence of ether in space. This was mainly because the analysis of the results of this experiment itself was classical (objective, as normally is the case in science) in nature i.e. there was no scope of or the feeling for the subjectivity either in the interpretation or in the underlying theory. It is quite possible that the concept of ether, ruled out once by the Michelson-Morley experiment, could be an essential component for the purposes of explaining the collapse of the wave function in quantum mechanics. Or, this ether of relativity theory could be a tanmātrā associated with the fifth mahābhūta ether (E_t) as the being b is also involved in the process of measurement. Alternatively, this ether of physics could be something which is beyond the range of physical instruments [36].

Any way the field of SO, and to some extent that of M, is so fine that one can never think of with this worldly I. Since they are beyond the concept of space and time and so are beyond the concept of any type of motion (disturbance) as the motion (e.g. the velocity, acceleration etc.) itself is derived from the space and time. As a matter of fact, the beings appear to be second quantized versions (i.e. a transition from continuous to a discrete form in the language of physics) of the field of SO alongwith some characteristic features of other fields like that of M. The field of M is not as global as that of SO. It may be remarked that any comparison of the fastest velocity known to physicists i.e. the velocity of light, with the propagation of these fields of SO or of M is meaningless. Similar is the fate of relative motion (an important input for the Michelson-Morley experiment). There is no concept of motion in the field of SO and to some extent in the field of M. These ideas about SO are further supported by Īśāvāśyopaniṣad [37] when it says :

aneja dekaṁ manso javīyo nainaddevā
āpnuvanpūrvamarṣat,
taddhāvato anyānatyeti tiṣthaṣminnayo mātriśva
dadhāti.

In other words, only the soul, not affected by itself, travels at a much faster pace than mind. It is beyond the domain of SE. In spite of being static (motionless), it supersedes all fast moving objects which can be thought of. In fact, the division of functions, full of attachment, of various essences of life, takes place only in the presence of Soul.

In the next verse, the same Upaniṣad further speaks, "*tadejati tanneijati taddūre tadvantike*" i.e. It (field of SO) moves, it moves not; It is far, and yet it is near.

4.3 Physical and nonphysical matter in the universe

What physicists have ever considered is the matter in isolation of the effect of b and more often also in isolation with the physical instrument used for the measurement. Although the limitations of the measuring instrument have been talked about in quantum mechanics for the last 70 years or so—in terms of uncertainty principle, but only recently questions have been raised regarding these limitations. The laws (like the probability law) derived basically for the inanimate objects, are used freely to understand the data pertaining to living beings (Schrodinger cat paradox etc.) without realizing the fact that the rules of dice cannot be the same as for the being. In fact, as we have seen [2] the being b is no more a simple object but a very complicated one having additional degree of free-will beside other essences of life. No doubt the physical laws, to some extent, have been able to take care of the interaction (limitations) of the measuring instrument with the physical object, but the interaction of the being b with the physical object, (either directly or through the instrument) could not be accounted for by these laws.

As a matter of fact, in view of the ideas presented in Sect. 4.2, the physical object in the presence of b cannot retain its same characteristics as it has in the absence of b. Therefore, we classify the inanimate matter of this universe as physical (henceforth called P-matter) and nonphysical or epiphysical [38] (henceforth called EP-matter). While the P-matter is governed by the laws of science in general or that of physics in particular, the EP-matter is basically the P-matter as perceived by the being b. As a matter of fact all animate objects come under the category of rather special EP-matter (or SEP-matter) (since they themselves have some or all essences of life including SO alongwith physical or biological body) and inanimate objects act as EP-matter in the presence of b only. In other words, if x is a P-matter then x + consciousness, is an EP-matter and x + consciousness + source of consciousness, is a SEP-matter. Though at much deeper level it might appear to be different but, for all practical purposes EP-matter can be considered as SEP-matter. This is mainly because the P-matter in the presence of consciousness gets "dressed" up at such a fast pace that it becomes rather difficult for it to distinguish between the field in which it is placed and the source of the field. Moreover, this "dressing" up also depends not only on the nature of P-matter but also on the nature of consciousness.

Thus, regarding the interaction between objects in this universe, following three possibilities can be thought of : (i) interaction between P-P, (ii) interaction between EP-P (or between P-EP) and (iii) interaction between EP-EP. It may be mentioned that the first possibility has been the subject of study, in the natural sciences for centuries (since the time of Newton) and the last two, naturally involve philosophy. Again, while the study of EP-P interaction is the subject matter of this and the next chapter and is partly described in Sect. 4.2, the discussion of SEP-SEP interaction is postponed to Chapter 6. However, a few remarks will be made about EP-EP interaction in the next Section.

This kind of classification will not only reduce the degree of confusion prevailing in some of the recent problems related to the measurement but also provide [39] a neater connection of science with philosophy. Keeping this type of classification in mind, we proceed in the next chapter to find an explanation of some of the problems raised recently in science.

4.4. Discussion

From the ideas presented so far in this chapter, it becomes clear that the relative consciousness is not only different for different beings but it could also be different for the same being at different space-time points. Further, the relative consciousness of different beings do not interfere as such unless the beings have cognizance of each other. In that case, however, the memory attributed to an action-at-a-time type force (cf. Chap. 6) comes into play. Perhaps, neither physicists nor bioscientists have yet realized this fact while talking of the role of consciousness in their data. Though we postpone such details to the next chapter, yet a few remarks about the interaction between the EP-matter particles are worth making here.

In this case again note the following possibilities :

(i) EP-E'P' interaction : Interaction between two different P-matter particles placed in the realms of different (relative) consciousness.

(ii) EP-EP interaction : Self-interaction of a P-matter particle placed in the realms of different (relative) consciousness.

(iii) EP-EP interaction : Interaction between different P-matter particles placed in the realm of the same (relative) consciousness (may be at the same or different space-time points).

(iv) EP-EP interaction : Self-interaction of a P-matter particle placed in the realm of the same (relative) consciousness which comes into existence at different space-time points.

Thus, the net effect of the relative consciousness of b on the P-matter particle is to enrich its own E, I, and M (essences of life) in terms of memory, intelligence and feelings (the corresponding acts of E, I and M) about P-matter, respectively. However, the absolute consciousness of b as such does not leave any effect on the P-matter. While postponing the further discussion of these ideas to the next Chapter, it is worth mentioning here about the direct and indirect measurements in science, in general and in physics, in particular. If the human being is directly involved in the measuring process of a physical quantity, we call it a direct measurement. On the other hand, if data is recorded by instrument(s) in one or more than one stage before it actually comes to the human being for analysis and interpretation, then it is the case of indirect measurement. Naturally, the latter case is a multi-stage process. The latter case will further be discussed in mathematical terms in Appendix B. Although the error analysis (systematic or otherwise) ensures the accuracy of the observations, but still the subjectivity (may be due to the relative consciousness) is bound to appear in the observations at the stage where the human being is associated with the measuring process.

[5]

Role of Consciousness in Scientific Observations

In spite of the fact that science has been a progressive discipline of knowledge for centuries and contents of some of its branches have grown up rather exponentially in recent times, there still remain [39] several unanswered challenging problems almost in every branch. In particular, physical and biological sciences are facing relatively more of such problems. While a complete understanding of the biggest (universe) and the smallest (elementary particles) in physics remains an open problem even today; the knowledge of a full-fledged mechanism and a justifiable reasoning for the explanation of the death or the birth of a human (animal) being is still desirable in biology, for example. Moreover, while other branches of science have only a distant connection with philosophy, it is the laws of physics which are akin to philosophy and applied these days even to biological sciences. In fact, there exist at present several multi-facet problems and phenomena in physics and biology whose basic understanding can require invoking of something which is beyond the domain of science, namely the concept of consciousness. In what follows, we point out some such situations in physical and biological sciences.

5.1 Consciousness in physical sciences

No doubt the role of consciousness in connection with the physical laws has been talked about by several physicists in the past but for a recent beautiful survey on this subject we refer to the work of Goswami [12]. With a view to finding an explanation in terms of the patomic model (cf. Chaps.3 and 4) and also for the sake of completeness, we briefly mention here some of the physical situations where the consciousness is expected to play an important role:

It may be mentioned that consciousness offers distinct effect on quantum (micro) and classical (macro) particles which, of course, represent the P-matter. In fact, the consciousness (or the interaction of the being b with these quantum or classical objects first through some or all the five SE's and latter through mind and intellect) while makes the classical particle to be physically realizable (manifestable), also allows the collapse of the wavefunction of the quantum particle at the same time. In other words, classical objects attain any or all of the five sense objects (namely smell, touch, geometry, taste, sound) in the presence of consciousness, whose existence in this world otherwise was not realizable. It may be remarked here that it is the consciousness which allows the compactification of higher dimensions in supergravity theories, thus providing a physically acceptable world.

In connection with the foundations of quantum mechanics and theory of relativity, several paradoxical situations are well known [40-42] in physics, for example, Einstein-Podolsky-Rosen (EPR) and EPR-Bohm paradox, Schrodinger cat paradox, the paradox of Wigner's friend, "Watched pot does boil" paradox, twin paradox. In fact, the apparent incompleteness (ignorance) of the predictive power of a theory leads to a paradoxical result. It does not mean that the theory on the basis of such a situation should be discarded, rather an explanation is needed to achieve perfection of the theory. While for the explanation of the twin paradox the involved relative motion between the reference frames has to be understood properly, for all the other paradoxes mentioned above the role of observer (or subjectivity) can offer an explanation or a clarification.

5.2 Problem of quantum measurement

Quantum measurement theory was proposed by Von Neumann [43] about forty years ago. According to this theory, the state of a quantum system undergoes change in two separate ways. The first is a continuous change completely predictable from the Schrodinger equation. The state spreads as a wave and becomes a coherent superposition of a number of well-defined ('potential') states allowed by the situation. Each well-defined state appears with a certain statistical weight given by its probability amplitude. On the other hand, the result of a measurement produces a discontinuous change in the state. All of a sudden the superposition while at one time offers multifaceted character to a well-defined state, *reduces* to just one actualized facet. One can visualize the state of superposition as the development of a pool of possibilities and the measurement process as a process of selection of one of the possibilities out of this pool.

When the above phenomenon continues, the mind-brain quantum system also develops in time and becomes a coherent superposition. The brain's functional machinery plays the role of measuring apparatus in the sense that it records the result of the collapse of the pure mental state, which otherwise is a coherent superposition. Before the collapse, the state of mind-brain exists again as a pool of tendencies. The collapse actualizes one of these tendencies leading to a conscious experience upon the completion of the measurement. Thus while the measurement is a discontinuous event in space-time, its outcome is a conscious experience.

Since we choose our conscious experiences to recognize a conscious experience as the outcome of the measurement process and yet we remain unconscious of the underlying process, it is this unconsciousness which pertains to self-reference and resolves into an illusion and thus arises the problem in quantum measurement.

As a matter of fact not only the method of accounting for the consciousness but even the consciousness itself is not properly understood in the conventional theories of quantum measurement. As emphasized earlier, the patomic model of the human being via the concept of relative consciousness can resolve this problem to some extent. Although the mathematical details involving these concepts are postponed to Appendix B, still a few ideas are worth mentioning here.

(i) *Collapse of the wavefunction :* While the conventional quantum mechanical framework has recently started exhibiting [44] its limitations from the point of view of applications to certain physical systems, its foundation has also been questioned from time-to-time. In the probabilistic interpretation (or rather formulation) of quantum mechanics, the wavefunction (also called probability amplitude) and its space and time evolution describes the motion of a material (P-matter) particle. In order that the particle be localized both in space and time the wavefunction must vanish at large distances. On the other hand, any quantum state (wavefunction) of the particle expressible as a superposition of a class of rather well-defined states (called eigenstates) instantaneously collapses or reduces to a particular well-defined state by way of suspending its evolution during the process of measurement. This feature of quantum measurement (popularly known as "collapse" of the wavefunction) while nurses the idea of an incomplete description of reality, also poses several questions regarding the "measuring" process itself. More often this feature of the collapse, attributed [40] to some uncontrollable interaction between subject and object or to the consciousness of the observer, has also been at the root of many of the paradoxes (see Sect. 5.1 above) of quantum mechanics.

Now the question arises as to why the wavefunction must collapse or vanish while the quantum particle does not cease to exist in the physical world? No doubt, the answer to this question is partly attributed to the limitations of the apparatus in terms of uncertainty principle, but the role of observer (or subjectivity in the spirit of Sects. 4.2 and 4.3) cannot be ruled out even if a perfect apparatus becomes available for this purpose. As it will be argued latter, the collapse is mainly due to the presence of observer (consciousness of relative nature) and is attributed again to some non-local effect for which apparatus cannot be held responsible.

(ii) *Hidden variables :* The concept of hidden variables proposed by David Bohm [45] about 40 years ago to bring out an alternative understanding of the quantum measurement problem, could not be appreciated as much earlier as it is done in recent times. According to Bohm, there are two orders of reality: the implicate order (the non-local realm of hidden variables) and the explicate order (the world of appearance). Further he believed in the existence of causal continuity of the two worlds. While Bohm's explicate order corresponds to the P-matter, the implicate order appears to be connected with the EP-matter in the spirit of Chap. 4.

5.3 Consciousness in biological sciences

The role of consciousness in biology is somewhat more transparent as compared to that in physics, mainly because it concerns everybody in day-to-day life through the phenomena of birth or death. While in the absence of consciousness (whether absolute or relative) the human (or animal) being is just like a P-matter, even in the presence of consciousness, most of the biological body can be described by biological or physical laws as mentioned earlier. The difficulty arises only when one invokes the question of consciousness i.e. the role of M, E, or SO in the language of patomic model. Even after a lot of advancement in biosciences it is not yet known from where does the consciousness enter during the phenomenon of birth or where it goes during the phenomenon of death. Even the intelligence (or memory) cannot be traced back inside the dead body of the being. In view of the patomic model, the intelligence or memory lies in the domains of I and E and they, in fact, are not retained completely during death. As far as the finest field of SO is concerned, in that one can visualize the process of quantization (i.e. the transition from continuous to discrete form or from infinite to finite) in connection with birth and its reverse with death (i.e. the transition from discrete to continuous form or from finite to infinite). These transitions take place more or less in an unnoticed manner.

5.4 Discussion and summary of chapters 4 and 5

With a view to understanding the relative degree of empiricism involved in physical and social sciences we have rather restressed the concept of subjectivity or consciousness in the light of Hindu philosophy in Sect. 4.1. This has also led to the idea of relative and absolute consciousness as used by other authors [12]. Within the framework of the patomic model of the human being and the *Pañcī-karaṇ*-Rule we have tried to understand the interaction of b with the physical world or *mahābhūtās*. As a result, we resort to categorize the matter of the universe in the form of P-matter and EP-matter. While the physical laws deal with P-matter, the latter can behave differently in the presence of b or of consciousness, thus converting itself into EP-matter.

Within the framework of the ideas presented in Sects. 4.1 and 4.2, it becomes possible to understand in a better way the limitations of scientific laws. While some of these limitations with reference to physical and biological sciences are pointed out and discussed, the solution of the problem related to the artificial intelligence in neural networks can also be tackled in the same manner. No doubt, some of the paradoxical observations in physics have started finding an explanation in the realm of consciousness, an explanation of similar observations in bioscience still remains a mystery. This is mainly because bioscientists hesitate in invoking something which is beyond the domain of science. But how long can such concepts be postponed ? In the years to come several other consciousness-manifesting-phenomena in physical and biosciences are bound to occur, whose explanations can be sought in patomic and not in atomic model. With reference to the limitations of the role of SE, M, I or E in the process of a physical measurement (observation) it is natural to ask whether one expects different uncertainty relations corresponding to these different essences of life. The answer is no; because these essences of life interact with a material particle rather coherently and produce a cumulative (combined) effect. As a result, it becomes rather difficult to extract the contribution of an individual essence. Further, this contribution of SE, M, I or E could be different for different beings. Therefore, the limits cannot be set on the perception of an individual being. This fact can, however, be noticed in social studies and in day-to-day life. In Hindu philosophy, this kind of ability of perception of an individual being is attributed to "*Prārabdha*" i.e. to the deeds of previous births (besides the deeds of this birth namely "*Sañcit*" and "*Kriyamān*"). In a way it is not difficult to understand this phenomenon in view of the patomic model. As mentioned earlier (cf. Sect. 4.2) it is not only the field of SO which undergoes the process of quantization during the birth (or during the transmigration of SO) but also the field of M alongwith a component each of I and E of the individual being participates in this process. We shall return to some of these points in Chap. 6.

It may be mentioned that several [46, 47] Western thinkers have also discussed the role of *mahābhūtās* and the associated tanmātrās in various physical theories. In these works, however, the concepts of *mahābhūtās* and tanmātrās are not used in their totality except for piece-meal-type citations. More often, they are wrongly identified [2, 47] with physical entities (e.g. partons are considered as *tanmātrās*). This is mainly because of the non-availability of a systematic framework for the human being and also for its interaction with the physical world. Perhaps the present patomic model in conjunction with the idea of Sect. 4.2, can offer such a framework.

To summarize our understanding about consciousness we mention the following : (i) absolute consciousness, as mentioned earlier, while is the characteristic of and originates from soul, its reflections from I, M or SE lead to pluralism or relative consciousness; (ii) consciousness is basically the (pure) quanta of the field of SO, but after combining with the field of M it forms *tanmātrās* in the presence of *mahābhūtās* ; (iii) as far as its role in sciences is concerned, its presence affects the P-matter by way of converting it into EP-matter. Further, in biosciences there seem to be certain phenomena involving the creation and annihilation of this pure quanta of consciousness without affecting the net field of SO. This, in fact, is in conformity with Īśāvāsyopaniṣad when it says [48]:

auṁ pūrṇamadaḥ pūrṇamidaṁ pūrṇāt
pūrṇamudacyate,
pūrṇasya pūrṇamādāya pūrṇamevāvaśiṣyte.

i.e. that (SO) is perfect and this (active part of SO) is also perfect, because perfect produces only perfect. And during the annihilation, the perfect (active part of SO) borrows perfectness from the perfect (SO) leaving behind the perfect (SO) again.

Appendix B : Mathematical Preliminaries

In Appendix A (cf. Chap. 3) we have made an attempt to write the Hamiltonian and the wavefunction for the being b within the framework of the patomic model, of course, under the highly simplifying assumptions. In the same spirit, here, we rather demonstrate as to how the interaction of a physical system (P-matter) and the measuring apparatus (human being included in the present case) can be investigated. For this purpose we use the available [29] formalism based on the Von Neumann theory of measurement and proceed with some additional assumptions. Again we consider the case of indirect measurement (cf. Chap. 4) of which the direct measurement case turns out to be a special one.

It may be noted that the present measuring apparatus now includes the human being with all essences of life (cf. Chap. 3) which turns out to be much more complicated than the one used in objective sciences. In fact, before the P-matter particle is finally realized by SO, all essences of life, in general, also play the role of measuring apparatus. Thus, besides the P-matter particle and the physical instrument, our system now consists of a series of other apparatus. As it is clear from Sect. 4.1, except for SO and WO, all other essences of life of the being, namely B, SE M, I and E offer a series of apparatus with successively increasing [2] the resolving (or rather realizing) power. As before, we do not account for SO and WO here since the former is the ultimate observer and the latter constitutes mainly the P-matter. In what follows, we present some technical terms and highlight the underlying assumptions made for such a description.

(i) *Pure states and mixture* : There could be both pure state and mixture description of an ensemble (P-matter). For a pure state, the entire ensemble is described by the same state vector $|\Psi>$, which can be expressed as a coherent superposition

$$|\Psi> = \sum_i a_i |\Psi_i>,$$

where the complete set $|\Psi_i>$, can be eigen states of energy, for example. The square of the coefficients $P_i = |a_i|^2$ gives the probability that a particular eigenstate in "potentia" is realized upon measurement. A mixture, on the other hand, consists of different pure states

$$|\Psi^{(1)}>, \quad |\Psi^{(2)}>, \ldots\ldots\ldots, |\Psi^{(n)}>,$$

already realized in the ensemble. The probability or weights of their occurrence being $w_1, w_2, \ldots, w_n$, respectively satisfy $\sum_n w_n = 1$. Here the weights w_i are the probabilities in the classical sense. The main difference between the two cases is that of the quantum mechanical description. In other words, in the P_i-description above, the phases of a_i remain indeterminate and it is this ignorance which proves to be the bliss of quantum mechanics. This is however not the case with the w_i-description to which the statistical interpretation of quantum mechanics is attributed. Further note that a measurement on a quantum ensemble normally converts a pure state into a mixture. For a mixture, one can again define the density matrix operator with several interesting properties and subsequently arrive at a more practicable description of the physical (quantum) system. We avoid such further details here.

(ii) From the Appendix A it can be noticed that the representation (A. 4) of the wavefunction Γ while can lead to a mixture (or w_i -) description, the representation (A.5) corresponds to a pure state (or P_i-) description. In the latter case, however, there exists a scope for accounting for the indeterminate concept like consciousness, provided Γ is assigned the meaning of probability amplitude.

(iii) The system consisting of a P-matter particle (P), the physical apparatus (PA) and the human being b, offers an example of the three-body problem in the language of physics. Further, the interaction Hamiltonian for this system, in general, can be written as

$$H_{int} = H_{b\text{-}P} + H_{b\text{-}PA} + H_{P\text{-}PA} \qquad \text{(B.1)}$$

Note that we have neglected the three-body interaction $H_{b\text{-}P\text{-}PA}$ here which can also be important (cf. Chap. 6) unlike what happens in physical science. In the conventional theory of measurement although some account for the $H_{P\text{-}PA}$ - term is made, but $H_{b\text{-}P}$-and $H_{b\text{-}PA}$-terms are either neglected or else their effect is attributed to some unknown (or uncontrollable) parameters (agents). To some extent, neglecting of the $H_{b\text{-}PA}$-term in (B.1) is justified since the measuring object is basically the P-matter particle and not the physical apparatus. However, in the actual situation, the human being, besides interacting with P and PA via physical (including action-at-a-distance type) forces (defined in terms of space-time concept and mainly attributed to B and SE in the language of patomic model) can also interact via action-at-a-time type forces through its M, I and E (see Chap. 6). In that case, $H_{b\text{-}P}$-term in (B.1) within the framework of the patomic model can be written as

$$H_{b\text{-}P} = H_{B\text{-}P} + H_{SE\text{-}P} + H_{M\text{-}P} + H_{I\text{-}P} + H_{E\text{-}P} \qquad \text{(B.2)}$$

where the terms $H_{B\text{-}P}$ and $H_{SE\text{-}P}$ account for the physical forces and $H_{M\text{-}P}$, $H_{I\text{-}P}$ and $H_{E\text{-}P}$ are responsible for the nonphysical forces. Since these nonphysical forces are capable of acting at the meditation level, the effect of $H_{M\text{-}P}$, $H_{I\text{-}P}$ and $H_{E\text{-}P}$ will be to enrich, respectively the feelings, intelligence and memory of the being about the P-matter particle. Thus, the total Hamiltonian for the system becomes

$$H_{tot} = H_P + H_{PA} + H_b + H_{int} \quad (B.3)$$

where H_b and H_{int} are given by (A.2) and (B.1), respectively and the Hamiltonian H_P and H_{PA} correspond to the P-matter particle and the physical apparatus. Broadly speaking one can also write H_{tot} as

$$H_{tot} = H_{phys} + H_{nonphys}, \quad (B.3)$$

i.e. as the sum of physical and nonphysical parts. Note that for H_{phys} the concept of space and time makes sense whereas for $H_{nonphys}$ it is not so; only meditation makes sense.

(iv) The states |B>, |SE>, |M>, |I> and |E> (cf. Chap. 3) now correspond to different apparatus (in the spirit of Von Neumann chain) in addition to the $|\phi_o>$ for the physical apparatus and $|\psi_o>$ for the P-matter particle.

(v) We have the meditation parameter μ corresponding to $H_{nonphys}$- part in the same way as the time parameter t corresponding to H_{phys}—part of H_{tot}. Further, while the physical measurement will affect the H_{phys}-part, the switching on of (relative) consciousness will however affect the $H_{nonphys}$-part. Also, corresponding to the Planck's constant $h/2\pi(=\hbar)$ in the physical part, we introduce a constant $g/2\pi(=\not{g})$ in the nonphysical part of H_{tot}.

Having introduced the above terminology, we are now in a position to demonstrate the effect of the interaction of a P-matter particle with the "complete" apparatus ("complete" in the sense that the human being is also included in the definition of the apparatus). If H_{tot} alongwith its pieces is hermitian, then, in general, the effects of measurement and consciousness together will appear [12, 43] through

$$\exp(-i\, H_{phys}\, t/\hbar - i\, H_{nonphys}\, \mu/\not{g})\, [|\Psi_o > |\phi_o > |B > \ldots . |E >].$$

in terms of phases of different varieties. If the second apparatus measures the first one, the third measures the second one, and so on, then for the state of the whole system (i.e. P-matter particle + Physical apparatus + human being), one obtains.

$$\Sigma_i\ C_i\ |\Psi_i\ |\phi_i > \ |B_i > |SE_i > \ |M_i > \ |I_i > |E_i >, \qquad \text{(B.4)}$$

which again is a coherent superposition within the framework of Von Neumann chain.

It may be mentioned that in this type of description of the quantum measurement there is no scope for any type of collapse (discontinuous or otherwise) or for the reduction of the wavefunction. According to Von Neumann our consciousness terminates the chain and a conscious state is never dichotomic. Since we have accounted for the consciousness to its inner-most existence (of course within the framework of the patomic model) in the human being, the question of collapse of the wavefunction in this case does not arise.

[6]

Interaction Among the Human Beings

Earlier in Chapter 4, we have defined the human being as a special EP. (SEP)-matter in the sense that human being is not only the P-matter present in the realm of consciousness of the self but is also a source of consciousness in itself. In this chapter, our aim is to study the interaction among the human beings and to look for an explanation of some of the exotic phenomena outlined in the Introduction. Also, a basis for statistical studies in social and allied sciences is suggested.

For this purpose, we again return to the long standing ideas of Hindu philosophy by introducing the existence of three forms of the human being, in the next section. It may be noted that in addition to the five *tanmātrās* described earlier, we need to introduce yet another variety of *tanmātrās* in Sect. 6.2 for the purpose of describing the SEP-SEP interaction. In Sect. 6.3, we study the effect of *pañca mahābhūtās* on the SEP-SEP interaction described in Sect. 6.2. As the role of mind (M) is found to be important in describing the SEP-SEP interaction, we discuss such a role in detail in Sect. 6.4. In Sect. 6.5, we extend the discussion of these ideas to the case of three and more interacting beings and highlight some of the difficulties in such a generalization. In a way, we suggest a basis for the working of statistical or empirical models for many-being systems in social and ecological sciences in Sect. 6.6. Finally, the ideas are summarized in Sect. 6.7.

6.1 Existence of three forms of the human being

No doubt the role of all the seven essences of life, namely WO, B, SE, M, I, E and SO of the human being should be considered at a given space-time point for a finer analysis of the behaviour, but some of them can be grouped together to make the subsequent discussion rather simple. Here, we consider the existence of three forms of the human being (b), namely gross-form ($\mathscr{G}$), micro-form ($\mathscr{M}$) and causal—form ($\mathscr{C}$) which are respectively known [49] as *Sthūl, Sūkshma* and *Kāraṇ* Ṣarīrās in Hindu philosophy. Under some simplifying assumptions and in the language of set theory these forms can be defined as

$$\mathscr{G} = \{SE, B, WO\}\ ;\ \mathscr{M} = \{E, I, M\}\ ;\ \mathscr{C} = \{SO\}.$$

Note that although SO manifests through all the three forms of b in terms of relative and absolute consciousness (cf. Chap. 4), yet it constitutes a separate set. In fact, the existence of the $\mathscr{M}$-and $\mathscr{G}$- forms is only through the $\mathscr{C}$-form in the background; whereas that of $\mathscr{G}$-form is first through $\mathscr{C}$-and subsequently through $\mathscr{M}$-form in the background. $\mathscr{C}$ is some sort of super or universal set. Further, in the absence of $\mathscr{C}$, the being b no more remains an example of SEP-matter.

It may be mentioned that the concepts of space and time in the sense of physics (or any objective science for that matter) exists only up to the level of $\mathscr{G}$ and beyond this, for $\mathscr{M}$ and $\mathscr{C}$, it does not make any sense, as mentioned earlier (cf. Chap. 4). As a matter of fact a more appropriate way of expressing these forms existing in this universe, is as follows

(i) $\mathscr{C} \cup \mathscr{G}$; (ii) $\mathscr{C} \cup \mathscr{M}$, in addition to the usual form

(iii) b $\equiv \mathscr{C} \cup \mathscr{M} \cup \mathscr{G}$

Note that in a realistic sense $\mathscr{M} \cup \mathscr{G}$ (or $\mathscr{M} \cap \mathscr{G}$) does not exist. Thus, while b is the perfect creation of God, the forms (i) and (ii) remain somewhat imperfect creations. As certain creatures in this universe do exist without M or I or E, or without all the three, they can be accommodated in the category of $\mathscr{C} \cup \mathscr{G}$; or else at the time of death a stage (may be for a few moments) comes when SO and $\mathscr{G}$ coexist and the rest $\mathscr{M}$= {E, I, M} disappears.

On the other hand, $\mathscr{C} \cup \mathscr{M}$-class of creatures is not expected to have any definite physical form in this universe though it is complete in all other respect. Perhaps, the so called ghost/spirit-class of entities in this universe can be put in this category. Clearly, for $\mathscr{C} \cup \mathscr{M}$-class of entities there are no boundaries of space, time and geometry. They are free to manifest, in general, through any physical object (P-matter). As these entities are devoid of interacting centres (i.e. mainly the senses of knowledge in SE) in response to *pañca mahābhūtās*, such a manifestation through an arbitrary physical object is not possible. In a way, it is in direct confrontation with *pañcī-karaṇ* rule (cf. Chap. 4). However, if this physical object happens to be a human/animal body then the infinite energy (in an 'inward' form) contained in these entities comes out through that body. This is what has been observed in several such incidences.

In accordance with these three forms of b i.e. $\mathscr{G}$, $\mathscr{M}$ and $\mathscr{C}$, there exist again three stages of human behaviour, namely *Jāgrat* (awakening), *Swapna* (dream) and *Susupti* (sound sleep). On the top of these three stages there still exists a fourth one called *Turīya*. This *Turīya*-stage is the one which b attains only after identifying itself with SO; otherwise most of the human beings in this world just pass through the first three stages in their normal life. In *Jāgrat*-stage all the three forms of b are present in a certain proportion in their active form and in *Swapna*-stage $\mathcal{G}$ is more or less inactive, whereas in *Susupti* not only $\mathcal{G}$ but also $\mathcal{M}$ is inactive and it is only $\mathcal{C}$ which remains active. An example of this latter situation could be the one when a person having a good sound sleep says in the morning that he indeed had a good sleep in the night. Once he was in sleep (i.e. both $\mathcal{G}$ and $\mathcal{M}$ were not in action) then how he is able to realize this fact is only due to the assimilation of b with $\mathcal{C}$ during the sound sleep.

In view of the above grouping of the forms of b, it is not difficult to find an explanation of some of the phenomena mentioned in Chapter 1. For example, (a) in the *Swapan*-stage, $\mathcal{G}$-form of b is not active and it is only $\mathcal{C} \cup \mathcal{M}$ (cf. the form (ii)) which is active and responsible for creating altogether a new world in the dream; (b) a Yogi in meditation who has controlled $\mathcal{G}$ after a certain practice, can again be in unison with $\mathcal{C} \cup \mathcal{M}$ and as well show the wonders to a common man not only by making predictions which are beyond space, time and geometry but also by creating materialistic items of a desired choice. However, in this latter case, the Yogi again acts against the laws of nature in the language of objective science and against the *pañcī-karaṇ* rule in the language of subjective science, which a Yogi is not normally supposed to do. (c) The above classification also supports the theory of rebirth in the sense that it is $\mathcal{C} \cup \mathcal{M}$ which transmigrates after death from one body to another. In fact, the appearance of this subset (ii) of b in a gross body is called birth whereas its disappearance from a gross body is called death. Since $\mathcal{M} \equiv \{E, I, M\}$, therefore, memory and intelligence alongwith some emotions are also passed on to the next body in the process of death. These characteristics appear as "*Prārabdha*" (cf. Chap. 4) i.e. as deeds of the previous birth. However, the nature of rituals at the time of death often does not allow this kind of transmigration of deeds in a materialistic sense. Still any lapse in these rituals leads to the cases where a person is able to recall his previous birth. As a matter of fact if $\mathscr{M}$ is detached from $\mathscr{C}$ prior to death (as is the case with a normal death) then the question of transmigration of deeds does not arise; Otherwise $\mathscr{C} \cup \mathscr{M}$ as a whole transmigrates (as is the case with an accidental death) into a new gross body. The fact that the newly born babies at the same space-time point have different degrees of intelligence and emotions, is a clear support to the above mechanism.

6.2 Interaction between human beings (bare case)

In spite of the fact that there cannot exist [50] any being (then what to say of the human being) in the absence of *pañca mahābhūtās*, we try to understand, as an idealized case, the interaction between the human beings in the absence of *pañca mahābhūtās* (bare case). For this purpose, we use the simplified version of the patomic model in terms of the three forms of b. Any effect due to the presence of *pañca mahābhūtās* on b-b interaction will be accounted for in the next Section. In a way here we ignore [51] the effect of *tanmātrās* τ_{ea}, τ_w, τ_a, τ_f and τ_{et} on the individual beings which, in fact, will keep b in communion with *pañca mahābhūtās*. We introduce here still a finer-class of tanmātrās to describe the b-b interaction.

Let the two human beings b_1 and b_2 characterized as $b_1 = \{\mathscr{C}_1, \mathscr{M}_1, \mathscr{G}_1\}$, $b_2 = \{\mathscr{C}_2, \mathscr{M}_2, \mathscr{G}_2\}$, be placed within the range of interaction. Though in the language of space and time this range is inconceivable, however, it depends on the degree of meditation (μ). Schematically, the b-b interaction is depicted in Fig. (4). This figure while drawn in analogy with the Feynman diagrams of modern physics, clearly describes the nature of b-b interaction in terms of five additional tanmātrās. These new *tanmātrās* are responsible not only for describing the varying nature of b-b interaction in terms of its subtle character but also for the behaviour of the beings.

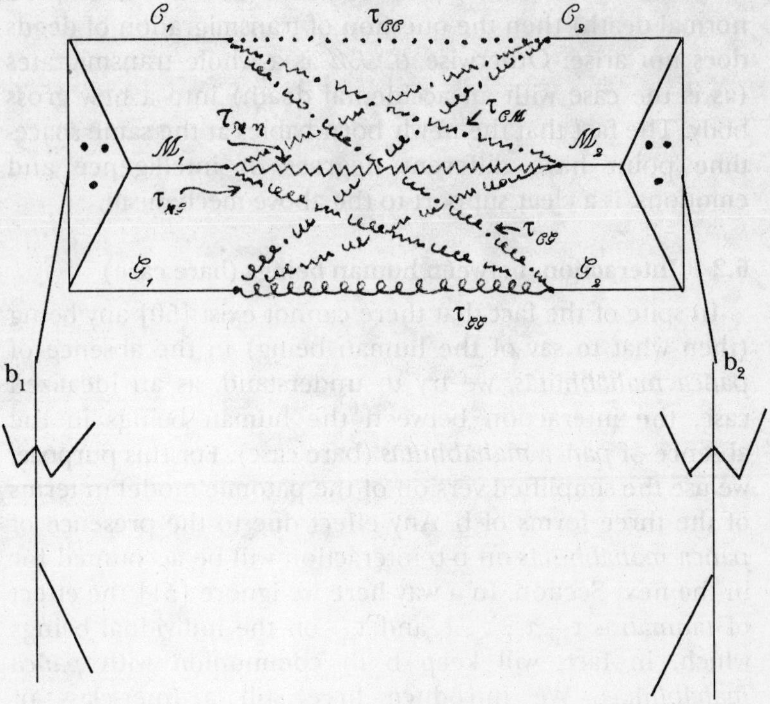

Fig. 4. Interaction between human beings

Before proceeding further it is worth reminding here some of the points pertaining to an individual being. In view of the fact that SO is the finest possible and all pervading field, $\mathcal{C}_1$ and $\mathcal{C}_2$ merely represent its quantized versions through b_1 and b_2, respectively. Further, the subsets $\mathcal{M}_1$, $\mathcal{G}_1$ of b_1 and $\mathcal{M}_2$, $\mathcal{G}_2$ of b_2 are active only in the presence of $\mathcal{C}_1$ and $\mathcal{C}_2$, respectively. Even for the interaction of $\mathcal{M}_1$ with $\mathcal{M}_2$ and $\mathcal{G}_2$, or of $\mathcal{G}_1$ with $\mathcal{M}_2$ and $\mathcal{G}_2$ (or vice versa), $\mathcal{C}_1$ and $\mathcal{C}_2$ remain in the background. Similarly, for the interaction of $\mathcal{G}_1$ with $\mathcal{G}_2$ (or vice versa), $\mathcal{M}_1$ (or $\mathcal{M}_2$ in the reverse case) remains in the background. In general, there exist nine more quanta (*tanmātrās*), namely $\tau_{\mathcal{C}_1\mathcal{C}_2}$, $\tau_{\mathcal{C}_1\mathcal{M}_2}$, $\tau_{\mathcal{C}_1\mathcal{G}_2}$, $\tau_{\mathcal{M}_1\mathcal{C}_2}$, $\tau_{\mathcal{M}_1\mathcal{M}_2}$, $\tau_{\mathcal{M}_1\mathcal{G}_2}$, $\tau_{\mathcal{G}_1\mathcal{C}_2}$, $\tau_{\mathcal{G}_1\mathcal{M}_2}$ and $\tau_{\mathcal{G}_1\mathcal{G}_2}$ corresponding to different possible interactions. Further, the universality of $\mathcal{C}_1$ and $\mathcal{C}_2$ implies that $\tau_{\mathcal{C}_1\mathcal{C}_2} = \tau_{\mathcal{C}_2\mathcal{C}_1} = \tau_{\mathcal{C}\mathcal{C}}$. Since each $\mathcal{C}_i$, $\mathcal{M}_i$, $\mathcal{G}_i$ (for i = 1, 2) is again a set in itself and as such for i = 1, they often will be in different frequencies as compared to that for i = 2. Therefore, it is reasonable to assume that

$$\tau_{\mathcal{C}_1\mathcal{M}_2} = \tau_{\mathcal{M}_1\mathcal{C}_2} = \tau_{\mathcal{C}\mathcal{M}};\ \tau_{\mathcal{C}_1\mathcal{G}_2} = \tau_{\mathcal{C}_2\mathcal{G}_1} = \tau_{\mathcal{C}\mathcal{G}};\ \tau_{\mathcal{M}_1\mathcal{M}_2} = \tau_{\mathcal{M}_2\mathcal{M}_1} = \tau_{\mathcal{M}\mathcal{M}};$$

$$\tau_{\mathcal{M}_1\mathcal{G}_2} = \tau_{\mathcal{M}_2\mathcal{G}_1} = \tau_{\mathcal{M}\mathcal{G}};\ \tau_{\mathcal{G}_1\mathcal{G}_2} = \tau_{\mathcal{G}_2\mathcal{G}_1} = \tau_{\mathcal{G}\mathcal{G}};$$

Further justification for the above assumption can also be attributed to neglecting the action-at-a-time type forces between b_1 and b_2. However, this is not so in reality. Thus, in all there exist 5 independent *tanmātrās* for the bare b-b interaction, besides $\tau_{\mathcal{C}\mathcal{C}}$ which is a universal quantum. The remaining five are $\tau_{\mathcal{C}\mathcal{M}}$ $\tau_{\mathcal{M}\mathcal{M}}$ $\tau_{\mathcal{C}\mathcal{G}}$ $\tau_{\mathcal{M}\mathcal{G}}$ and $\tau_{\mathcal{G}\mathcal{G}}$ which respectively are shown by in Fig. (4).

In order to describe b-b interaction in terms of these five *tanmātrās* the meditation (mental situation) plays an important role. While $\tau_{\mathcal{C}\mathcal{C}}$ may corresponds to the *Turiya*-stage of b, $\tau_{\mathcal{C}\mathcal{M}}$ or $\tau_{\mathcal{C}\mathcal{G}}$ corresponds to the stage when the micro-or the gross-form of b_1 is in direct communion with SO of b_2 and vice versa. Again they correspond to different degrees of meditation. As a matter of fact it is the relative consciousness manifesting through M, I, E and finally through SE and B of the one being which is responsible for the interaction with the other being. In fact, minds of b_1 and b_2 through their acts of meditation play crucial role in this whole process of interaction. We shall return to these details in subsequent sections. Alternatively, the consciousness of one of the beings in tune with its mind, is capable of activating the different essences of life of the other being. During the meditation of middle level when $\mathcal{G}$-

form is the least active, the relative consciousness through $\mathcal{M}$ dominates the b-b interaction via $\tau_{\mathcal{MM}}$

It may be mentioned that the physical sciences account only for the interactions mediated by $\tau_{\mathcal{GG}}$ and that too in the absence of consciousness. Only recently, scientists have started [52] realizing the role of consciousness and that of $\tau_{\mathcal{MG}}$ in the context of quantum measurement problem as discussed in the previous chapter. No doubt the role of space and time is more pronounced up to the level of $\tau_{\mathcal{GG}}$, however it reduces as one proceeds to the label of $\tau_{\mathcal{MG}}$. Beyond the domain of $\tau_{\mathcal{GG}}$ not only the action-at-a-distance type forces are important but also an account of action-at-a-time type forces (through the memory as an act of E) becomes essential for a better comprehensibility of the roles of $\tau_{\mathcal{MG}}$ and $\tau_{\mathcal{MM}}$. These $\tau_{\mathcal{MM}}$ -type forces are responsible for explaining the exchange of concepts like memory, intelligence and emotions between the beings. For an understanding of the b-b interaction in totality, the meditation plays a distinct role. It is responsible for the introspection of the self and subsequently for the inward part of the human energy. We shall return to this point later.

6.3 Interaction between human beings in the presence of pañca mahābhūtās (dressed case)

An alternative way to describe the interaction between human beings is in terms of human-aura. In fact there exist a human-aura surrounding each human being which is different for different human beings in the sense that the degree of development of the essences of life for each being is different. When the question of interaction of two beings arises, then their human-auras having different degrees of fineness, interact. While the interaction of SO is universal (independent of space and time), the interaction of other inner essences (like E, I, M) is not only state-dependent but also becomes much more transparent through the process of meditation (an act of mind, M, characterized by the parameter μ). However, the interaction between the $\mathcal{S}$-forms remains confined to the surface level.

As mentioned earlier in Chapter 4, the human being perceives the *pañca mahābhūtās* first through SE and B and finally through M, I, E. As a result when two human beings interact in the presence of *pañca mahābhūtās* all the *tanmātrās* of the previous section (bare case), in principle, get affected. However, $\tau_{\mathcal{CC}}$ still remains subtle and all the rest get "dressed" up by the presence of the *pañca mahābūtās* in the same way as the *tanmātrā* associated with a particular *mahābhūta* gets "dressed" up by the presence of the remaining four *mahābhūtās*. Since b-b interaction is also of action-at- a- time type in nature, it hardly matters whether two persons first shake hands and then recognize each other or else first recognize each other and then shake hands. Recognition while partly attributed to the memory (an act of E), also depends on the meditation or the tuning of mind.

Since each being interacts with pañca mahābhūtas through the *tanmātrās* τ_{ea} τ_{w}, τ_{a}, τ_{f} and τ_{et} (cf. Chap. 4) to its inner-most level; therefore, when such a being interacts with another similar being the *tanmātrās* $\tau_{\mathcal{CM}}$, $\tau_{\mathcal{CS}}$, $\tau_{\mathcal{MM}}$, $\tau_{\mathcal{MS}}$ and $\tau_{\mathcal{SS}}$ get accordingly "dressed" up to become $\vec{\tau}_{\mathcal{CM}}$ $\vec{\tau}_{\mathcal{CS}}$ $\vec{\tau}_{\mathcal{MM}}$ $\vec{\tau}_{\mathcal{MS}}$ and $\vec{\tau}_{\mathcal{SS}}$ respectively. As a matter of fact the five external *tanmātrās* τ_{ea}, τ_{w} τ_{a}, τ_{f} and τ_{et} interact with each human being through five interacting centres, namely through nose, tongue, ear, eyes and skin, respectively. As a result while $\mathcal{C}$ of each being remains unchanged, $\mathcal{M}$ = {E, I, M} of each being accordingly get enriched in terms of memory, intelligence and feelings with respect to *pañca mahābhūtas* though in different proportion. Consequently the bare quanta $\tau_{\mathcal{CM}}$ $\tau_{\mathcal{CS}}$ $\tau_{\mathcal{MM}}$ $\tau_{\mathcal{MS}}$ $\tau_{\mathcal{SS}}$ get dressed up and the b-b interaction becomes modified as compared to the bare case.

It may be noted that the bare *tanmātrās* (τ's) could be more or less the same for all pairs of human beings but the dressed *tanmātrās* (τ, s), may differ for each pair in the sense that the *pañca mahābhūtās,* which basically interact through B and SE, definitely affect M, I and E of each being. Moreover, this effect, in general, is different for different beings. If one also accounts for such a difference then the assumption made in the previous Section (namely, $\tau_{\mathcal{C}_1\mathcal{M}_2} = \tau_{\mathcal{C}_2\mathcal{M}_1}$ or $\tau_{\mathcal{M}_1\mathcal{G}_2} = \tau_{\mathcal{M}_2\mathcal{G}_1}$ or $\tau_{\mathcal{C}_1\mathcal{G}_2} = \tau_{\mathcal{C}_2\mathcal{G}_1}$, etc.) breaks down.

6.4 Roles of mind and sub-conscious mind in the b-b interaction

Before discussing the case of more than two interacting beings, we first recapitulate the roles of M, I and E for an individual being. It is true that the presence of *pañca mahābhūtas* not only affects SE, B and WO with respect to a being, also its $\mathcal{M}$-form and subsequently its existence gets affected by them. Further, only through the meditation, it can be realized that the transition from $\mathcal{M}$-to $\mathcal{C}$-form is mainly attributed to E (i.e. the ego of a micro nature at the subconscious level) and that from $\mathcal{G}$ - to $\mathcal{M}$-form it is attributed to M. While the former transition could be smooth, the latter turns out to be more crucial in the sense that this transition is from the external (materialistic) to the internal (spritualistic) world. In fact, M in conjunction with the relative consciousness is capable of taking a position in all or in any of the essences of life starting from WO to SO. While M is an observer for the external world, it is also a realizer for the internal world at the same time. Since M has more than one role to play, all its actions with reference to the human being are complementary.

Several methods and systems have been described [53] in Hindu philosophy for controlling the mind and subsequently for obtaining the state of Yoga. By Yoga we mean the path of becoming the being, b, in unison with SO by overcoming the states of M, I and E. As a matter of fact M is a very powerful and peculiar kind of essence of life. While this itself is controlled by its own vigilant part (i.e. the part which is in unison with I), it is capable of controlling all lower substates like SE and B including the WO. Religious scriptures [54] in many ways and a number of saints of different creeds have been hinting at the methods of controlling the mind from WO and sense objects, but at the same time also suggesting the methods to applying it to higher objects i.e. towards SO. In spite of the fact that the vigilant part of M can be activated either by meditation or by self-observation, in its absence M has the tendency towards downward fall. Once M has a position in a particular sense of knowledge, then that sense of knowledge is also able to empower the intellect. As a result whole of the logic moves around that particular sense object.

Not only this, it is the mind which allows the perception of *pañca mahābhūtās* in this universe; it is the mind which creates altogether new worlds in the *swapna*-stage; it is the mind which is responsible for all kinds of lively acts during the *Jagrat*-stage. In fact, it is the mind which regulates all the activities by controlling senses of knowledge and action. These are some glimpses of the role of mind with reference to a human being. In summary, it is only the mind which is responsible [55] for all kind of attachments and bondages in this world on the one hand, and for the liberation of soul ("*Moksha*") on the other, as it is vividly said [56] "*manasā kalpyate bandho mokshaste naiva kalpyate.*" Our aim is not to elaborate on these ideas further here but to emphasize the role of mind in b-b interaction.

Since M is capable of taking a position in any of the essences of life in a human being, the interaction of this being, with another one turns out to be of highly complicated nature. In general, all essences of life of the one being can interact with all the essences of life of the second being. Not only this, the interaction is also of both action-at-a-distance and action-at-a-time type. Therefore, even if the beings are not in a physical contact or not even having the cognizance of each other, they are able to interact on the basis of their memories (i.e. due to E). This type of interaction, is one of the finest possible interactions between the beings. Next comes the category when the beings do not have the physical contact but only the cognizance of each other. In this case all the three, M, I and E, (in their micro-form) can play their roles in the b-b interaction and accordingly the beings can share the feelings, intelligence and memories. This type of interaction is of somewhat lower level as far as the fineness is concerned. Third category of the interaction comes into play when the beings also have physical contact in terms of SE, B and WO. In this case, however, the beings can share sense objects, physical actions and worldly objects to maximum degree in addition to the feelings, intelligence and memories to somewhat lesser degree. This category may also involve the concept of space and time.

It may be mentioned that when two beings are present any of the three categories of b-b interactions described above can come into play. But it mainly depends on occupying the position by M in the essences of life of one of the beings and also on the tuning of the same or the different essence of life by M of the other being.

6.5 Case of three or more interacting human beings

After accounting for the pairwise two-body interactions in physical theories, very little scope is left for the effect of three—or higher-body forces. Here, however, it is not so. When three human beings are present, then not only their pairwise interactions but also the three-being interactions are equally important. This is partly due to the fact that the b-b interaction has a distinct feature i.e. it has also a action-at-a-time type character, contrary to the known physical interactions. Moreover, there is no concept of time arrow here beyond a certain stage. In spite of the fact that M of each of the three beings can occupy a place in any of the essences of life of the corresponding being, for any communication or interaction among the beings these M's should be in tune with each other. More often this tuning not only of M's of different beings, but also with respect to different essences of life becomes a problem for understanding the interaction. The magnitude of this problem further increases if the number of interacting beings becomes larger. Further, the relative consciousness could also be of varying degree for different beings. Thus, in general, b-b-b interaction also turns out to be a complicated one. The magnitude of this underlying complexity in this generalization can further be demonstrated as follows:

Let b_1, b_2, b_3 be the three human beings with correspondingly labelled essences of life. If M_1 of b_1 occupies a place say in I_1, then M_2 of b_2 and / or M_3 of b_3 should also occupy the places in I_2 and /or I_3, respectively in order to have a meaningful b-b-b interaction; otherwise the interaction may not be of b-b-b-type. More appropriately, in that case the interaction may be of SEP-EP-EP or SEP-SEP-EP type. In fact, in the absence of the relative consciousness in any of the other two beings, in general and in any of their essence of life, in particular, the corresponding being or the essences of life will appear as an EP-matter for the interacting first being. In this case, however, the nature of interaction becomes quite different, mainly a restricted one, as described in Chapter 4. The following simple arithmetical estimate further reveals the nature of the complexity involved, for example, for the b-b interaction:

Note that besides [57] WO, M_1 of b_1 is capable of interacting through 23 vertices of interaction (these are 10 senses of knowledge and action + 5 sense objects + 5 mahābhūtās + M + I + E = 23) with the other being. Naturally, M_2 of b_2 also has the same number of interacting vertices and in a realistic case the number of interacting frequencies could be 23 x 23 = 529. This number becomes even larger if three or more beings are interacting. No doubt by considering the three-forms of existence of the human being (cf. Sect. 6.1) some simplification on this front could be achieved but that will be at the cost of accuracy. In other words, the three-form description of the b-b interaction still remains an approximate one.

6.6 Emergence of statistical description for many-being systems

We have seen that the magnitude of the complexity of the interaction among human beings increases with increasing number of the interacting beings. No doubt for these many-being systems, b-b interaction still remains in the background but at the same time many-being interactions are equally important. Social or ecological sciences offer examples of such many-being systems. As in physical theories few-body approaches fail to explain the many-body systems and statistical approaches are found to be more useful for this purpose, here also similar is the case. Though the details of such many-being systems will be discussed in the next chapter, a few points are worth mentioning here.

In physics while the knowledge of the basic force-law (whether it is an electron or a nucleon many-body system) is available alongwith the characteristics of the interacting particles, here however such force-laws are not yet precisely known in the case of the systems under study. As far as the characteristics of the interacting beings are concerned, to some extent, they are established in Chapter 3. Regarding the study of many-being systems a lot of work has been done in recent years in social and ecological sciences. Based on statistical data, empirical models are developed for the purposes of these studies. For the reasons which will be discussed in the next chapter, the predictive power of these models however remains restricted as compared to those of statistical or empirical models used in objective sciences. Also, some of the ideas prevailing in social sciences are based on the centuries old experiences of the human race. Further, these experiences, besides the environmental factors, have also been changing with respect to space and time. In view of the fact that the data in social sciences involve a certain degree of subjectivity in terms of the free-will of the human being, the predictive power of the corresponding models cannot be as good as that in objective or natural sciences. Moreover, the laws of statistics derived from the inanimate dice may not be applicable as such to a system of animate objects.

In connection with the existing studies in social sciences it is rather interesting to mention one more analogy with the physical theories. In atomic or nuclear many-body systems in physics, the explanation of the underlying phenomena is sought mainly in terms of valence electrons or nucleons, respectively. The contribution of the inert core is often neglected. Similarly, in social sciences the data collected for the statistical/empirical description of a phenomena also pertains mainly to SE and B levels alongwith WO of the patomic model. The effect of inner essences of life of the human being is somehow not taken into account in an objective manner and to some extent it is not possible also. No doubt, SE, B and WO of the patomic model can play the roles of valence particles of physical theories but at the same time the roles of inner essences of life is also very important unlike that in physical theories. Actually this is the stage from where enters the subjectivity in the data of social sciences.

6.7 Discussion and summary

With a view to understanding the behaviour of the human being vis-a-vis its interaction with other beings, use is made of the patomic model of Chapter 3. A simplified version of this model in terms of the gross-, micro- and causal-forms of the being has further helped in understanding not only the bare b-b interaction through five additional *tanmātrās* $\tau_{\mathcal{CM}}$ $\tau_{\mathcal{CG}}$ $\tau_{\mathcal{MM}}$ $\tau_{\mathcal{MG}}$ $\tau_{\mathcal{GG}}$ but also through the dressed one. The latter case deals with the b-b interaction in the presence of *pañca mahābhūtās.* An explanation of several exotic phenomena is found within this framework. While the description of b-b interaction is relatively found simple, three- or many-being interactions turn out to be complicated. The underlying complexities are clearly illustrated. It is suggested that the role of mind (M) and that of subconscious mind (E) is very important during the transitions from $\mathcal{G}$-to $\mathcal{M}$-form or from $\mathcal{M}$- to $\mathcal{C}$-form. Their roles in two-and many-being systems are also emphasized. Further, for any meaningful interaction among beings the tuning of minds not only of different interacting beings but also of their different essences of life is essential.

While the ideas presented here are in their most absolute terms, still their applications down to the level of behavioural sciences are intentionally avoided. However, in this context the following remarks are worth mentioning: No doubt the interaction among the human beings comes into existence when their minds are tuned through 23 vertices for each. Now the question arises as to what type of this interaction is going to be useful either to the mankind as a whole, in general or to a society, in particular. As a matter of fact the nature of this interaction could be of both types i.e. constructive or destructive, in the sense of standard norms established by various religious faiths. The constructive interaction could be the one which can, not only provide pleasure (the best of the downward extreme i.e. WO) but also peace (the best of the upward extreme i.e. SO) in the language of the patomic model; whereas the destructive interaction is the one which provides just the opposites and the worst of extremes. It may be noted that there has to be some sort of harmony between peace and pleasure not only with respect to an individual but also with reference to a many-being system. In fact, this should be the ultimate outcome of the interaction not only of an individual being or of a pair of beings with *pañca mahābhūtās* but also of a collection of beings i.e. of a society as a whole. Opening and closing verse of Kathopaniṣad has beautifully summarized the nature of universal, constructive b-b interaction when it says

> *auṁ sahanāvavatu. saha nau bhunaktu. sahavīryaṁ karavāvahei. tejasvināvadhītamstu. mā vidvisāvahei. auṁ śānti! śānti ! ! śānti ! ! !*

meaning thereby "Let Him protect us both. May He Bless us with Bliss of knoweldge. Let us exert together. May what we study be well studied. May we not hate (quarrel with each other). Om peace ! peace! peace!!!"

[7]

Modelling in Science and Religion : A Unified Approach

In the present times both models and the process of modelling have played an important role in the understanding and the description of several abstract and intriguing ideas occurring frequently in different disciplines of knowledge ranging from humanities [58-60, 62, 63] to pure sciences [11, 61]]. On the other hand, the concept of models in its varied form have also been prevailing in almost all religions and faiths of the world for thousands of years. In spite of the fact that a model, howsoever close to reality it may be, cannot be the reality itself; models have become an inseparable part in the description of reality. As a matter of fact various cults in religion and different disciplines of knowledge in science, often differ merely on the basis of models or on the underlying process of modelling, as a result of which there exist a division of races, societies and scientists as well.

In the next section, we argue that there exists a common objective for both religion and science. Then, we briefly describe the models used in religion and social sciences in Sect. 7.2. In Sect. 7.3, we continue with such a description of models used in science in general and in natural and mathematical sciences in particular. The process of modelling is analyzed in Sect. 7.4. The quality of a model is discussed in Sect. 7.5 in purely philosophical terms. In Sect. 7.6, the idea of the contingent plane used by Holton [64] to characterize the analytic and empirical dimensions of a scientific thought, is generalized to a contingent space. This accommodates the ideas of Holton as a special case of the present scheme of the unification of religion and science. Further, in Sect. 7.7, it is established that scientists are also idol worshippers in actual sense, in the same way as a priest in religion. Finally, in Sect. 7.8 we summarize our ideas.

7.1 Do religion and science aim at common objective ?

No doubt the true or absolute reality is one and only one. It is not only independent of a model-based description but is also a matter of realization only. Still, different religions have been presenting and hinting to this reality differently from time to time. Further, the realization of this reality has been possible only to certain individuals (known as saints, yogis or prophets in different religions) who have awakened their human faculties to the greatest extent. To a common man, however, various models of the reality (depending not only on space, time and race but also on circumstances) have been presented at different points of history. Models in science have also described reality which is, however, of somewhat different nature. Although the realities as perceived through the religion and as described by the science could be the same in certain limits but they manifest differently at different levels of human faculties.

In fact in science the quality of a model and the reality it describes ultimately depend on the nature of the data it explains [65]. Again, among various branches of science, only biology and physics seem to play an important role in the description of true or absolute reality. These days, while biosciences still have to answer the challenging questions relating to life and death, physics at its foundation level itself has started accepting [12] the role of consciousness in the understanding of certain data pertaining to measurement whose explanation otherwise seems impossible.

Now the question arises as to whether there exists a possible framework to assimilate these ideas of religion and science in a unified manner or at least to throw light on the domains of science and religion with reference to the description of absolute reality. The answer very much relies on the understanding of the common factor i.e. the human being itself. As a matter of fact the modelling of this rather complicated common factor is necessary. There is hardly any religion of the world (except Hindu philosophy) which throws light on the description of the human being itself in a more concrete form. While human being with all its faculties is the ultimate observer or measuring instrument in sciences (particularly in physics), it is also an ultimate realizer of any kind of reality of religion. In fact, the human being (or a society in its collective many-body or pluralistic form) has played (and is still playing) a dual role: as a realizer of a subjective reality or a propounder of a religion and also as an acceptor of an objective reality or a propounder of scientific laws.

In the present chapter, our efforts will be to look for a unified description of the realities described above in the context of religion and science within the framework of the patomic model of the human being proposed in Chap. 3. In particular, the origin of certain models popular in science and religion, the quality of a model with reference to its predictive power, and the process of modelling will be discussed in their most absolute terms. In fact, the disciplines contributing to model-based knowledge can broadly be classified in two major categories namely, (i) humanities and social sciencies, and (ii) pure sciences and technology.

7.2 Models in humanities

While the model of a particular religion or faith promises peace to an individual human being, it provides certain place-value in a society. Since the society is a collective version of individuals, the models on which a social system works cannot be independent of the models of the religion accepted by that society. On the other hand, scientific advancements also leave some impact not only on the society but also on the religion if the latter is not of orthodox-type. In view of the fact that a society and its acceptance of a religion is a function of both space and time; the ideal model of a religion should either already have built in set of universally accepted postulates or else an acceptance to constructive criticism necessary from time to time in view of the scientific advancements.

7.2.1 *Models in religion*

For the purposes of describing the role of a religion to an individual or to a society one can think of three components of a religion, in accordance with Hindu philosophy. These components are [66] : *Jnān* (knowledge), *Upāsana* (methodology) and *Karma* (action or practice). The quality of a model in religion can be characterized by the relative magnitudes of these components present in that religion. A model of a religion is said to be perfect if all the three of its components exist to their highest degree of perfection and with a consistent and self-explanatory logic. Somehow, this is not the case with most of the religions of the world when they are looked upon from this point of view. In fact, while all actions should be in accordance with an ideal methodology, the latter itself should lead to the attainment of knowledge of supreme i.e. the knowledge of self (SO).

No doubt the action and methodology components of a religion could vary with respect to space, time and circumstances but the knowledge component; if it is an ideal one, should be independent of these factors. Unfortunately, most of the religions of the world (except the Vedic philosophy) do not have an ideal knowledge-component. As a result their foundation remains weak and the so-called leaders of that religion always try to defend it by all means to prevent its eventual extinction. Common mass of people, as and when realizes this fact; always goes for a change of faith in such a situation, if left to their free-will. Alternatively, there exists a natural desire in the human being for a faith in order to attain peace. If the given faith does not serve the purpose, then a common man is forced to change the faith.

A true religion cannot be a localized one in space and time. On the other hand, if a religion originates from an individual and at a certain point of time then that religion cannot be a universal one: mainly because either there was no human race or there was no desire for peace of the common mass before the birth of that individual. Only thing an individual prophet or a saint actually does is either to supplement or to revive the underlying ideas of a religion at a certain point of time. Within this framework, however, none of the religions of the world (including the major ones which perhaps are defined by the number of followers) turns out to be a universal one except for the religion described in the Vedas. Further, the number of believers cannot be a criterion for the quality of the model of the religion.

Though it is difficult to compare and remark about different religions of the world without actually practising them (and that is not possible in a single birth alone!), still a ground-level-comparison reveals that most major religions of the world (except the religion described in the Vedas) have limitations in terms of space and time. Better the methodology and knowledge-components of a religion, longer it is going to survive. In what follows we present some important features of the models of major religions of the world for the sake of comparing their relative merits :

(i) *Buddhism* : Founded by Lord Buddha (500 B.C.) in India; It has boundaries of space and time; works on 8 basic postulates; peace of mind is supreme and hence good methodology and action-components; Followers practice Yoga and meditation and believe that people are born and reborn over and over again; when they achieve enlightenment they are finally freed from all desires and the cycle of rebirth; Buddhism is a subset of Hinduism.

(ii) *Christianity* : Founded by the followers of Jesus Christ (after 4 A.D.); In spite of its geographical expansion it has time boundaries. As such no definite postulates except those dictated by Church, however denominations have some and practise them accordingly; No deep knowledge-component; Methodology is more of mechanical nature; no definite ethical norms in practice; Followers believe in one God and in Jesus Christ as the son of God.

(iii) *Confucianism* : Founded by Confucius (king Futzu) (6th century) in China; Followers believe in heaven, ancestor worship and many gods; Also, believe in after life with ancestors in heaven.

(iv) *Hinduism* : Neither exact date nor exact founder is known; several prophets and saints had contributed (and have been contributing) and revived this religion from time to time; There exists a kind of perfect knowledge—and methodology—components in spite of maximum degree of variations in action or practice-component both in space and time; There is a scope for all-round development of human faculties in the methodology. Hinduism is not a religion but a life-style with maximum degree of flexibility and accommodating capacity on the one hand, and presenting ideals to every aspect of life on the other; This idealism is not only logical but more often scientific in nature.

(v) *Islam* : Founded by Mohammad (622 A.D.) in Medina; It has space and time boundaries and it is based on

5 postulates, namely belief in Allah, prayer 5 times a day, donating to charity, fasting from sunrise to sunset during the month of Ramzan, making a piligrimage to Mecca at least once in a lifetime; methodology is more of mechanical nature and rigidity in practice or action-components; Followers believe that their bodies die and their souls live forever in heaven or hell.

(vi) *Judaism* : Founded by Abraham (5000 years ago); it has space-time boundaries; Followers believe in one God, Jehovah, who is the creator and ruler of the universe; also, believe that souls will live forever.

(vii) *Shinto* : Founded in antiquity and influenced by Confucianism and Buddhism; shin means "way of spirit." Followers believe that all human beings are the offsprings of nature, so whatever they think or do must be natural and therefore right; Shinto worship consists of keeping on good terms with numerous Gods.

(viii) *Taoism* : Founded by Lao-Tze (600 B.C.) in China; space-time boundaries exist; Tao means "a way or a road;" Followers believe in the Yin and Yang of the universe; Yin represents the earth and Yang represents the heaven; The balance of Yin and Yang gives order to the world; People are encouraged to work in harmony with nature.

From the above summary it appears that (i) all religions do believe in the existence and universality of soul and (ii) out of these eight models, four (particularly those practised in the eastern-part of the world—Japan and China, namely, Buddhism, Confucianism, Shinto and Taoism) are already accommodated in Hinduism at the methodology-level. With due apology to readers of other religions it is worth mentioning that none except Hinduism offers a perfect degree to all the three-components of a religion. In Hinduism the knowledge-component is so perfect that it offers a complete and an ideal description for a naturally accepted life-style at all space and time points in spite of several deviations in recent centuries. Moreover, it offers a full-fledged theory (not limited by space and time) for each of the actions of and by the human essences (cf. Ref. (2)) of life.

7.2.2 *Models in social sciences*

As the details of this subject are beyond the scope of the present book, we shall restrict ourselves here only to the philosophical aspect of the models used in social sciences instead of their finer details.

As mentioned before that a society is a collective version of individual human beings, for the sake of its survival any set of norms have to be based on the religion accepted by that collective version. Further, this faith or religion is not only going to reflect on the norms but also in the model for a society. Besides the religion, there are several other factors which affect the modelling of a social system; namely, political, economical and geographical. Further, scientific advancements also play an important role in this process. In fact, with a view to improving the existing models of a society lot of research is going on these days in rigorous mathematical terms. Very often the modelling is done in an empirical manner and the laws of statistics (derived from an inanimate object like dice) are applied to various types of predictions. It may be mentioned that laws of dice may not be applicable to the society consisting of human beings. As a result, the predictive power of sociological models has to be low as compared to that of science.

As far as the laws of science and those of statistics (derived mainly for inanimate objects) are concerned they cannot be applied as such to a society for the following reasons : (i) each human being in spite of its complicated structure, also has a reacting power (in terms of free-will) at different levels, (ii) the natural phenomena on which the survival of a society depends are still not within the control of scientists. Therefore, the models used for a society are more of subjective nature contrary to the models used in science. We shall return to these details later.

7.3 Models in science and technology

For the sake of a systematic and planned development of a society in scientific terms, these days several governments in the world are funding the modelling in science and technology. While the modelling in science has been prevailing since its origin, the modelling in technology has started only recently [58]. As a matter of fact the relation between the modelling in science and technology is the same as that between the modelling in religion and society. The modelling in technology cannot be independent of that in science. As several specialized books [61] and reviews [11] are available on this subject, here we shall touch upon only some philosophical aspects of modelling phenomena in these areas.

The idea of modelling is very common to almost all branches of science. Whenever there appears a deeply involved phenomenon in nature about which a variety of data (sometimes from different sets of experiments) becomes available, scientists start thinking of a possible framework within certain set of postulates in order not only to explain these data but also to predict some new results. As for the postulates, they are normally the basic requirements (principles) taken almost as god-given facts. No doubt, in recent years some philosophical objections have been raised against some of these postulates (see for example Ref. [67] in relation to physics) yet their validity remains unquestionable within certain boundary-lines.

While there exist only countable models in biology or chemistry, every branch of physics abounds in models of various natural phenomena. In fact, in the process of modelling the role of mathematics is also crucial; larger the extent to which it can be applied to understand the underlying phenomenon, better becomes the model in terms of its predictive power. While mathematics has become an inseparable part of a model in physics or in chemistry, its role in biosciences has also been emphasized recently [61]. With a view to putting the knowledge in a nutshell or to carry out a certain type of abstraction, these days even highly advanced and modern mathematical methods are employed in framing certain type of models in physics. For example, string models of field theories are expected to unify the four fundamental interactions of physics.

It may be mentioned that a theory in science plays the same role as a model in religion. As a result, it becomes rather natural to classify various models in science in the same way as the models in religion, i.e. in terms of the three-components. Thus, the models in science can also be classified as knowledge ("*Jnān*")-based (J-category models), methodology ("*Upāsana*")-based (U-category models) and experiment ("*Karma*" or action or practice)-based (K-category models). Though all the models in science in general and in physics in particular describe objective reality in one way or the other, their relative merits in this respect are, however, different. In other words the models which can bring the observed reality closest to the absolute reality can be placed in J-category models. On the other hand, the models which offer alternative ways to describe the same observed reality can be put in the U-category models, and the models which are phenomenon - based can be put in the K-category of models. It may be noted that the degree of abstraction or rigour decreases as we go from the models of J-category to K-category. As illustrative example of this classification-scheme, we pin-point some cases below, from physics:

While there exist numerous examples from almost every branch of physics for the models of K-category, relatively less number exists for the models of U-category. Examples for the models of the J-category are even rarer. Sometimes the ignorance about the underlying dynamics of a system also leads to different models for that system. For example, there exist many models for the atomic nucleus or for the elementary particles for that matter and not for the atom itself. Although there exist several examples for J-category models (like those of quantum mechanics, relativity, classical and quantum field theories etc.) in physics, still a single example of atomic nucleus will make the above classification clearer. For the nucleus in spite of a large number of phenomenon-based (K-category) models (like liquid drop model, shell model, fermi gas model etc.) known to explain its various properties, several mathematical technique in terms of two-body forces (U-category of models) are used to explain the same set of properties. However, if one ignores the finite boundary and considers the nucleus as an infinite nuclear matter, then the field theoretic models of strong interaction (models of J-category) can be applied to explain at least some of these properties. Similar situations very much arise in atomic, solid state and plasma physics.

It is just a coincidence that the present scheme of classifying the models in science is in conformity with the one proposed by Verma [68] for the research in science. In fact, according to Verma, a scientific concept consists of three parts namely, *mantra* (knowledge), *tantra* (system or methodology) and *yantra* (experiments) and all the three parts are equally important for a complete understanding of a scientific phenomenon. The importance of these three components in the present context is already emphasized above.

In order to make science useful to mankind technology comes on the way. As a matter of fact while the pure science gives birth to technology, the nourishment of the latter in a country depends on many local factors like economical, sociological, industrial, geographical etc. These factors are used as input parameters for the modelling in technology.

Further, the output or the predictions of these models are used as feedback to improve upon the overall development of the society or the country. In other words, some sort of optimization is done between the input and the output results. In view of the fact that social and geographical factors also play the important role, as a whole the modelling in technology turns out to be a complicated mathematical problem.

7.4 The process of modelling

Having presented a unified framework in terms of the three-components (knowledge, methodology and practice or action) for the models in both religion and science, we analyse here the actual process of modelling in terms of the patomic model. There also exists some sort of analogy between religion and science as far as the designing of a model is concerned. In fact, while in both the role of ego (E) is common, the idea of modelling originates from the level of I with a certain set of postulates. In practice, however, this idea reflects at SE, B and WO level in case of religion and at SE, B and scientific instrument level in case of science. Finally, the society becomes the laboratory in case of religion and technology or nature becomes the laboratory in case of science for the purposes of testing these models. Depending upon the dominance of any of these faculties of the human being in this process, the category of the model can be decided.

In other words, the limitations of human faculties (like E, I, M, SE and B) and also of scientific instrument to understand, to explain or to describe the "infinite," normally leads to the process of modelling in both religion and science. While the "infinite" ("*samasti*") is the matter of self-realization only, its manifestation in a "finite" ("*vyasti*") form again with a set of postulates is actually the modelling process. In fact, this "finite" representation (of the "infinite") has different meanings at different levels of human faculties. For example, if this "finite" is designed at the level of E and I then this will lead to the origin of J- or U-type models (cf. Sect. 7.3) in science and a particular type of ideology in a religion. On the other hand, if this "finite" is designed at the level of SE, B or scientific instrument level then this will give rise to K-type models in science and action or practice-dominated models in religion. Furthermore, while E, SE and B contribute uniformly to the models of both religion and science, M dominates the models in religion and I dominates the models in science.

It is interesting to note that some sort of reversible process is going on in religion and science as far as the manifestation of the absolute reality is concerned. Subjective and objective realities, in fact, appear to be the two sides of the same coin—absolute reality. In religion, while subjective reality comes out in the form of objective reality, in science, however, objective reality goes in, in the form of subjective reality. In these processes however the human being with all its faculties acts as an instrument i.e. as a realizer of the subjective reality in religion and as an observer of the objective reality in science. The models, of whatever level they may be, just carry a certain fraction of the "infinite"—absolute reality. It may so happen that the realities outside (outer world) and inside (inner world) are the same and the instrument of the human faculties is not able to realize the oneness of these two realities, perhaps due to its imperfection. This is what Hindu philosophy emphasizes [69] through the universality of soul (SO) with all its characteristics like omnipresence, omniscience, omnipotence etc. Further, in the spirit of Īśāvāsyopaniṣad [70] "*tandantarasya sarvasya tadu sarvasyāsya bāhyataḥ,*" which means "It (absolute reality) is within all this and It is outside all this." It may be mentioned that there exists a micro-component of ego at this stage which prevents from identifying the realities of religion and science with the absolute reality.

In the language of three-world concept the absolute reality also appears to be over and above the three worlds. In fact, in order to understand the reality described by science the three-world concept has been prevailing [13] for some time in the philosophy of science. The world described by the models of physics is the physical world, the world perceived by the human being is the mental world and the world which really exists is the conceptual world. Now, it is not difficult to translate this concept of three-worlds into the above rather more logistic framework of patomic model.

7.5 Quality and limitations of a model

Although from the classification-scheme discussed in Sects. 7.3 and 7.4, the degree of quality and limitations of a model in religion or in science are clear, still a few remarks are necessary from the point of view of patomic model.

To be specific, the quality of a model no doubt judged by its predictive power, is however inversely proportional to the number of postulates necessary in framing the model. Again, if the postulates also vary with space, time and/or circumstances then this further reduces the quality of a model. All this, as a whole, is a complicated mechanism since human faculties also play their role besides the above factors. However, in science if a model has a large predictive power but with very few technological applications then it can be said to be a good model. On the other hand, in religion if a model, in spite of the best predictive power does not have a bigger society of its followers, cannot be said to be a good model. In a realistic sense this should not be the case. But this is how the human faculties play the role in establishing the quality of a model.

As mentioned before, the models in religion are M (mind) dominated whereas those in science are I (intellect) dominated, still the peace derived (by a scientist in case of science and by a priest in case of religion) from the models is the same in its absolute sense mainly because both have the taste of the same absolute reality although in different forms.

As far as the limitations of a model either with respect to its predictive power or with respect to realization or description of reality are concerned, they are different in all the four cases (namely, religion : society :: science : technology). While the limitations of models in religion are already emphasized in Sect. 7.2 and those of society and technology are well-known, the limitation of models in science can be pointed out here. In fact, the laws of physics have often been questioned [67] when they are used for animate objects who possess some degree of free-will as well.

In these years, the mathematization has become an art of bringing a particular discipline of knowledge on the forefront. While natural sciences were already dwelling on this art, humanities and biosciences have also entered into this game, recently [58, 61]. Naturally, any limit on the mathematization is bound to set a limit on the modelling process [71]. Until recently not much was known about the nonlinear mathematics. Even after its advancement there have been some practical difficulties in its application to various branches of science. On the other hand, theoretical understanding of several newly discovered [72] phenomena in physics, chemistry and other sciences (like biology, geology, atmospheric science etc.) now requires an account not only of nonlinearity but also of anharmonicity and noncentral nature of the underlying forces. As a result, the solution of a realistic problem becomes somewhat more complicated. These recent observations are not only going to affect the models of U- and K-category but also of J-category. The computers can however be helpful in this respect but only for the models of U- and K-categories as they themselves have limitations in terms of thinking process. As a matter of fact they can only share the assimilative and deliberative parts of the human thinking and not the important creative part. These are only the human faculties which can have creativity in absolute terms. In such circumstances the models of J-category also have the limitations irrespective of the fact whether they belong to science or humanities.

7.6 A generalization of the contingent plane

Earlier Holton [64] and recently Mitra [73] have used the concept of a contingent plane to classify the nature of scientific thinking, in general and of physical theories, in particular. This contingent plane, basically is a x-y plane in which the empirical character of a scientific thought is depicted along the x-axis and its analytic character along the y-axis. Further, on this x-y plane the concepts of science appear as the points and the hypotheses or the propositions of science as the curves. To account for various dimensions of thought (also called "thematic" dimensions), Holton brings in the third z-axis on this plane. Thus, the contingent plane becomes a subset of a 3-dimensional space. On the other hand, Mitra realizes the existence of many logical and mathematical systems requiring, in turn, a severe degree of selectivity regarding the analytic dimension. In other words, the y-dimension is much less unique than the x-dimension. Also, the role of non-contingent (thematic)-dimensions is enphasized by Mitra.

In view of the existence of several logical systems for the analytic character of a scientific thought, it seems that the objective content of this thought is not completely taken care of by the x- and y-dimensions of the contingent plane. As a result, the non-contingent (thematic) dimensions are also expected to carry a certain fraction of the objective content of the scientific thought. In such a situation, it would be rather encouraging to generalize the idea from a contingent plane to a contingent space. This can be done by extracting that particular dimension of thought out of the noncontingent dimensions which is responsible for the objective content and accordingly by depicting it along the z-axis. The other remaining dimensions of thought can still be attributed to an extra (hyper) dimension which, in turn, will now completely account for the subjective content of the scientific thought. At this stage, however, there exists a direct correspondence, respectively between these x-, y- and z-axes of the contingent space and the K-, U- and J- categories of models/theories discussed in the present chapter. Interestingly, this idea of the contingent space can also be extended to the case of models in a religion as well. Besides the points and curves in the contingent plane, one can now also think of solid figures in the contingent space. Which, of course, very much depends on the underlying theory/model.

As mentioned before, the J-category of models also has limitations from the point of view of understanding the absolute reality. Therefore, whatever is left unaccounted for by these models (particularly the subjective content) in the present context, can be attributed to the hyper-dimension of the generalized contingent space.

7.7 Are scientists idol worshippers ?

Now, we return to the question of idol worship in different models in religion. In a particular model, an idol is basically the geometrical representation of the "infinite" into a "finite" form at the level of SE, B and WO. In this connection a parallelism from the modern theories of physics namely, Kaluza-Klein type supergravity theories [74] is worth mentioning. There, infinite-dimensions are compactified to finite dimensions by generating some physical properties (like mass, charge etc.) from the missing dimensions. A similar thing can be visualized in case of idol worship. As emphasized in other (cf. Chap. 4) context, the interaction of the human being with the physical world is possible if the essences of life are in tune with the external world in terms of consciousness. Thus, for a certain class of followers, J- or U-component of a model are not realizable/ perceivable, hence for them the "finite" geometrical idol or picture-portrait is representing the invisible "infinite."

Also, in science, a scientist assumes the "infinite" by a "finite" with some postulates and adopts all sorts of methodology to have a communication with different experiments. However, the analysis of data is such that he never violates the rules of the "idealized" model framed at a higher level. In a way, the scientist is also a worshipper of "finite"—may not be consisting of a geometrical shape but a "finite" of higher-(intellect-) level. In this way scientists are in no way less than an idol worshipper namely, the priest of a religion.

7.8 Discussion and summary

With a view to understanding various models and the processes of modelling prevailing in both religion and science, a common framework is suggested in terms of the Hindu philosophy. The role of the human being in terms of its patomic model is analysed in this regard. The role of the human being is found to be two-fold: one as a realizer of subjective reality of religion and the other as an acceptor of the objective reality of science. Again, for the purposes of classifying various models of religion and science a very general, common framework is suggested in terms of the three-components of a model. In other words, all models are placed in three major categories: knowedge-based (J-category), methodology-based (U-category) and action-practice- or experiment-based (K-category). In fact, whichever component dominates the designing of the model, the latter is placed in the same category. While several analogies in terms of the understanding of religion and science together are derived, it is emphasized that models of a society cannot be independent of the models in religion accepted by that society. Also, in the same spirit the models of technology in a country cannot be independent of the models in science provided local and geographical factors are taken into account (cf. Sect. 7.3).

In both religion and science, the models initially originate from an individual, then accepted by a group of so-called experts and later propagated or established by the followers (or experiments). Although rare, but converse also happens as history reveals. In fact, whenever there is a desire to bring order in a chaotic behaviour of a society or to search an order in the accumulated experimental data, the latter happens. In the recent past while both space and time are contracted by the advancement of science and technology, there have been attempts to look for universal norms (beyond the domain of various cults or religions) for the mankind. Now the question arises as to which of the religions can provide such universal norms for the whole mankind. In view of the fact that almost all (major or minor) religions of the world are based on a certain type of models with space-time-boundaries, such universal norms can only be deduced either from the basics of all religions or from the Vedic philosophy. In spite of so many models in Hinduism, the main root of all i.e. the Vedic knowledge, appears to be free from modelling as far as the descriptions of nature and life are concerned. Perhaps for this reason only the Vedic knowledge has been surviving for centuries. As pointed out earlier (cf. Sect. 7.2), the Vedic knowledge is not a religion but a life-style, complete in itself and does not involve any basic postulate in its purest form. To summarize, it may be emphasized [75] that "we have just enough religion to make us hate, but not enough to make us love one another."

[8]

Further Applications of the Patomic Model

Although several applications of the patomic model of the human being are already enumerated qualitatively at various places in this book, but their quantitative studies with reference to behavioural sciences as also in the context of other disciplines are still desirable. Here, we highlight some further applications of this model:

8.1 Social sciences

As the patomic model can be used to study several ecological problems in a more precise manner, its applications to social sciences can appear in two distinct ways : (i) As mentioned earlier, one can consider the society as a collective version of the individual beings and apply the laws of statistics on this ensemble. No doubt such studies have already been going on these days, but within the framework of the patomic model it becomes possible to estimate the corrections to these studies arising mainly due to the essences of life, perhaps in a quantitative manner and thereby providing the results to a better degree of accuracy; (ii) As mentioned in Chap. 6, starting from the individual being and its interaction with other beings, theories can be developed for a many-being system more or less in the same manner as it is done in physics in the context of many-body theories. Such quantitative studies, may turn out to be more difficult in the absence of any analytic form of the interaction between the beings, however, it would provide better accuracy in the predicted results. The latter approach suggests an all together a new style of studying the social sciences. The main differences in these two ways of studying a many-being system is that in the first case it is many-to-one approach whereas in the second case it is one-to-many approach.

8.2 Psychology and parapsychology

In general, psychology deals with the studies of the role primarily of the mind in the human behaviour in the existing birth alone, whereas the studies concerning the role of mind, intellect and ego of the previous birth(s) in the behaviour of the present birth of the human being, can be considered to fall under the discipline of parapsychology. While psychology has been a regular subject of study for a long time now, parapsychology has not yet carved out its proper place in this respect. This is mainly due to the fact that the scientific advancement has not only suppressed the growth of this subject due to nonavailability of a logical reasoning for rebirth, but sometimes the factual verification of the events also becomes a problem. The test cases have been there in the past, they exist even today and perhaps will be there in future. There are plenty of examples of rebirth. As emphasized earlier, the phenomenon of rebirth can be understood in terms of the patomic model i.e. in terms of the transmigration of micro-along with causal-body at the time of death (cf. Chap. 6). Since micro-body consists of M, I and E, it is possible to investigate within this framework, the relative proportions of the feelings, the intelligence and the memory transmigrated during the process of death; or as to the manner in which this proportion gets affected by the changes of mode of death.

After discussing the role of mind in Chap. 6, there is no point in elaborating here the applications of the patomic model with reference to psychology. The patomic model is, in fact, capable of pin-pointing clearly the role of mind in human behaviour vis-a-vis that of other essences of life.

8.3 Scientific epistemology

The part of the scientific thinking which has an overlap with philosophy, is normally termed [22] as scientific epistemology. Among various branches of science, physics seems to have a somewhat bigger overlapping region in comparison to other branches of science. In fact, the foundation of the laws of physics can easily be sought in the realm of philosophy. As discussed in Chap. 2 and noticed from the discussions in subsequent chapters, it becomes much easier to study the scientific epistemology within the framework of the patomic model.

As a matter of fact the patomic model offers a systematic framework to identify the limits (or to seek the domain) for the validity of the laws of science. Beyond these limits, the laws of science would, naturally, require some sort of generalization or sometimes an alternative working scheme to accommodate the roles of M, I and E (see e.g., Sects. 7.4 and 8.5).

8.4 Causality principle in physics

No doubt there exists a cause for every effect. Now the question arises as to which level (in terms of essences of life) the effect of the cause is noticed or at what level the corresponding cause existed prior to the showing of the effect. Within the domain of physics the cause is very much there in terms of four fundamental forces and the corresponding effect appears either in the form of some physical process (or in the form of some "action"). As emphasized earlier (cf. Chap. 6), in physics one deals only with action-at-a-distance and/or contact-type forces. As a result the causality principle in physics is stated basically in accordance with the arrow of time i.e. cause is always followed by an effect. If the time-arrow changes the direction the process also gets reversed. For example, the creation of particles in the forward-time can be considered as the annihilation of particles in the backward-time. Logically, these two (processes) cases are supposed to be equivalent in physics. In fact, the spirit of the causality principle in physics is essentially carried through the equal-time commutators of the observables.

From the point of view of physics the above ideas are consistent and make sense as long as one does not invoke the concept of action-at-a-time type forces in the underlying process. But some of the processes we have talked about in this book definitely involve this concept and as such require a more generalized type of causality principle of which the causality principle of physics should appear as a special case. It is true that the causality principle of physics is expected to be valid for the processes taking place at the level of SE and B. Beyond these states, within the framework of the patomic model, this principle requires reconsideration.

In Vedānta philosophy two types of *Kāraṇ* (causes) of an act, in general, are described [76], namely "*Nimitta*" and "*Upādān.*" The often cited example is that of a potter who makes the vessel from clay. While the clay, in this example, is said to be the "*Nimitta*" *Kāraṇ* for making the pot, the potter himself, on the other hand, is said to be the "*Upādān*" *Kāraṇ*. In other words, the "*Upādān*" *Kāraṇ* is more essential than the "*Nimitta*" *Kāraṇ*. It may be mentioned that physics through the causality principle deals only with the "*Nimitta*" *Kāraṇ* and does not account for the "absolute" causes i.e. the way in which the four basic forces of physics are held responsible for the occurrence of the physical event or the process. In other words, physicists do bother only for the answer to "how" and not that to "why" in establishing the laws. The latter will ultimately bring in the role of "Creator" in the description of laws. This is how the domain of laws of science is defined. In general, the subjectivity is avoided as far as possible in science.

It is not necessary to talk of "*Upādān*" *Kāraṇ* (or the absolute cause) next to the "*Nimitta*" *Kāraṇ*. Like subjectivity (cf. Chap. 4), cause can also be relative and absolute. Before actually bringing in the role of absolute cause (i.e. the ultimate "creator"), the "*Nimitta*" *Kāraṇ* can be of relative character according to its origin from M, I and E. Particularly, the interaction of M (and naturally that of SO also) is more subtle than that of SE and B (which are mainly responsible for the physical forces). Therefore, before accounting for the field of SO, the fields of M through E require *a priori* consideration through the concept of action-at-a-time type forces.

8.5 Action principle in physics versus Yoga of action

In physics the invariance of the "action" integral with respect to the Lorentz (space-time) transformation, in the form of Noether's theorem, has led [77] to several interesting results concerning the origin and the nature of the physical laws. As a matter of fact the evolution of the physical process in space and time always taking place in such a way that the physical action in the process attains the minimum value, has further led to an interesting mathematical equation which describes most of the present day classical dynamics and field theory. Now the question arises as to what is the relevance of these so called "basic" principles of physics in the context of the Yoga of action as described in the Vedānta philosophy ? Or, conversely, in what way the Yoga of action has a connection (if any) with these laws of physics ? Before we look for an answer to this question within the framework of the patomic model, a few points are worth remembering at this stage regarding the domains of the two disciplines, namely the physical science and the science of the self (Yoga):

(i) Motives in the two cases are different. In physics while one tries to understand nature in a nut-shell through the action principle, the Yoga of action as described [78] in Srīmad Bhagavad-Gītā, on the other hand, is meant for attaining the peace of the highest degree in spite of all involvements in the physical world. In fact, in the process of following the Yoga of action all inward-processes are set in order and hence reducing (or leaving) the entropy of the system (in the language of physics) either to a constant or to its minimum value.

(ii) In view of (i), one can again ask "how the inner system (consisting of SE, M, I and E) by following the Yoga of action can be put in order ?" Indeed it is the most difficult task to do or to observe in practice in all its perfection. But the underlying theory of the Yoga of action helps a lot through a sequence of stages in attaining such an order. Naturally, the most ordered actions will correspond to minimum investment of energy (efforts) to attain the same goal in day-to-day life. True, depending upon an individual, to some extent we all use our logic (intellect) in minimizing the efforts (at inner or outer level) but only temporarily i.e. it may be for a particular action and sometimes only in an unknown manner. On the other hand, if one does not observe the Yoga of action, his/her actions are likely to be disordered or chaotic meaning thereby wastage of energy (whether inner or outer) for the same constructive output. Naturally, the Yoga of action is meant only for the human being.

Within the framework of patomic model or according to Yoga of action M of the human being regulates the actions of SE; I keeps a watch on these actions of both M and SE through its act of intelligence. Experiences gained in this manner are stored in the memory as an act of ego E. Now the question is how these actions of SE, M, I and E can be performed so that the being b performs the upward transitions (cf. Fig. 1) in the direction of attaining the peace in spite of remaining in the field of WO all the time. This art or the style of living is beautifully described in the Vedānta philosophy.

As far as the principle of least action is concerned it is very well valid even for the above actions of M, I and E, but its manifestation in the physical sense appears only at the levels of B and SE i.e. at the stage where from the role of space and time becomes important. In human behaviour it is observed [23] that one wants to do minimum (may be at the physical level) with an idea of maximum attainment. Although there is often a balance between inward (i.e. of M, I and E) and outward (i.e. of SE and B) actions in the sense that if one is less the other is larger or vice-versa, but sometimes in some beings this balance is found to be disturbed. This kind of imbalance can be attributed to the deeds of previous birth i.e. to "*Prārabdha*". Details of the theory of Yoga of action are left to the interested readers.

Finally, in the spirit of the Appendix B, one can as well write the total Lagrangian as $L = L_{phy} + L_{nonphys}$, in the same way as the Hamiltonian and can consider the extremization of the generalized action

$$S_{gen} = \int L_{phy}\, dt + \int L_{nonphys}\, d\mu,$$

where the contribution to the first term mainly comes from the work done in term of physics and to the second term comes from the inner actions of M, I and E i.e. mainly from the Yoga of action.

arrangement (cf. Fig. 11) in the direction of attaining the peace or state of remaining in the field of WO all the time. This art of the style of living is beautifully described in the Vedanta philosophy.

As far as the principle of least action is concerned, it is very well valid even for the above actions of M, I and E, but its manifestation in the physical sense appears only at the levels of B and S, i.e. at the stage where from the role of space and time becomes important. In human behaviour it is observed [53] that one wants to do minimum (may be at the physical level) with an idea of maximum achievement. Although there is often a balance between inward actions of M, I and E and outward (i.e. of S and B) actions in the sense that if one is less the other is larger or vice-versa, but sometimes in some beings this balance is found to be disturbed. This kind of imbalance can be attributed to the deeds of previous births (or 'Prarabdha'). Details of the theory of Yoga of action are left to the interested readers.

Finally, in the spirit of the Appendix B, one can as well write the total Lagrangian as $L = L_{phy} + L_{inner}$, in the same way as the Hamiltonian and can consider the extremization of the generalized action:

$$\delta S_{tot} = \int L_{phy}\, dt + \int L_{inner}\, d\tau$$

where the contribution to the first term, which comes from the work done in terms of physics and to the second term comes from the inner actions of M, I and E, i.e. mainly from the Yoga of action.

[9]

Conclusions : Does the Progress in Objective Sciences Lead to Truth ?

Before we actually highlight the main outcome from the studies of the proposed patomic model and its limited applications, it is better to have a nut-shell summary of all the preceding chapters.

After emphasizing the need for a discipline like subjective science for the purposes of having (i) a better understanding not only of the overlapping region between philosophy and science but also of behavioural sciences, (ii) an explanation of several exotic phenomena for which the objective sciences have no explanation whatsoever, and (iii) a common framework for the unified description of religion and science, in Chapter 1, a brief survey of the existing knowledge concerning the human being and Nature is made in Chapter 2. A discussion of life, matter and their inter-connection is also presented there in scientific terms.

Using the essences of life as ingredients, the proposed patomic model for the human being in Chapter 3, not only helps in understanding some of the abstract philosophical ideas, but also throws some light on the domains of physics and philosophy. In view of this it becomes possible to make certain remarks on the identification of partons (of physics) with the *tanmātrās* of Hindu philosophy. In fact, this chapter has formed the basis for the discussions in all subsequent chapters.

In Chapter 4, the interaction of a physical (= material) particle with the human being within the framework of the patomic model is discussed. As a first step in this direction, technical terms like "subjectivity" and "objectivity" (synonyms of absolute and relative consciousness, respectively), "physical" and "nonphysical" matter, and so forth, are introduced for the purpose of discussing the role of consciousness in scientific observations. The interaction of the human being with *pañca mahābūtās* is also discussed there in great details. As a continuation of these ideas, the role of consciousness in scientific observations in the context of physical and biological sciences is highlighted in Chapter 5. In this chapter, an attempt is also made to understand the collapse of wave function in quantum mechanics, the compactification of dimensions in quantum field theories and the process of perception of classical objects within the framework of the patomic model.

The interaction among the human beings is understood, in Chapter 6, by using a simplified version of the patomic model i.e. by introducing the concept of existence of three forms of a human being (b), namely gross-, micro-and causal-forms in accordance with the *Sthūl*, *Sūkshma* and *Kāraṇ Ṣarīrās* of Hindu philosophy. This has offered a possible framework, in which an explanation of several well known exotic phenomena such as experiences at the time of death, description about ghosts/spirits or about previous birth and similar other parapsychological experiences can be found. It may be noted that the objective sciences have no explanation for any of these phenomena. A need for additional five *tanmātrās* (quanta of interaction) is emphasized there in order to describe the b-b (being-being) interaction more on the lines of the Feynman diagrams of modern physics. In the presence of *pañca mahābhūtās* these new *tanmātrās* while getting "dressed" up, do offer a description of the realistic situation. Attempt is also made there to generalize these ideas to understand the three- and many-being interactions. However, the underlying difficulties in this type of generalization to many-being systems further suggested a basis for the origin of statistical/empirical models used frequently in social or ecological sciences in the same way as is the case with many-body theories of physics.

In Chapter 7, we further looked for a common framework in terms of the patomic model to understand the degree of *reality* as described by science (objective reality) and realized in a religion (subjective reality) through various theories/models. The role of three common components (knowledge, methodology and practice in accordance with *Jnān, Upāsanā* and *Karma* of Hindu philosophy) of each—a theory in science and a model in religion, is emphasized for the description of these realities. Also, the process of modelling is understood uniformly in both science and religion within the framework of the patomic model. It may be emphasized that in both religion and science, the models framed at the level of intellect and ego are very instructive and not widely different from each other except for a few postulates; however they become distinct and different with a larger set of postulates at the level of mind and body only. In view of the fact that a scientist always looks for those interpretations of his observations (data) which do not violate the basic postulates of his idealized model (scientific theory), it is pointed out there that he is in no way less than an idol worshipper i.e. the priest of a religion.

Although we have explored some important aspects of the patomic model of the human being in Chaps. 4-7, there still remain a lot more for investigations, besides those indicated in the last chapter. In fact all those disciplines of knowledge which directly deal with human (or animal) essences of life, are bound to involve the patomic model at certain stage and the latter can offer a quantitative understanding of that discipline. As far as the qualitative description of several recent phenomena in physics from the point of view of Vedānta philosophy is concerned, it is beautifully summarized by Swami Jitatmanand in a recent publication [79].

An understanding of the human being, preferably in terms of models has become now essential for several reasons; for example (i) for pursuing any type of quantitative study about the behaviour of human (or animal) being, (ii) for defining limits on objective sciences from the point of view of understanding the absolute reality, and (iii) for the purposes of establishing certain principles (if at all possible) on which the subjective science of philosophy can be developed in more rigorous terms like the objective sciences. Patomic model, based on the Vedānta philosophy and discussed in this book, is one such attempt in this direction.

No doubt the role of consciousness has been argued in the context of quantum measurement, the reality is that the consciousness is a pre-requisite for or an important ingredient in the "complete" measuring process (cf. Appendix B) of any physical quantity. In particular, at that stage of measurement where the human being is involved, the role of consciousness is more pronounced. Only thing is that the scientists have to go somewhat beyond the domain of the laws of science. In near future many more phenomena in objective sciences may emerge whose theoretical understanding might require a somewhat stronger role of consciousness.

In spite of the fact that the laws of science have much deeper meaning (i.e. beyond the domains of SE, B and WO) somehow their testability and subsequently the applicability is restricted only to phenomena analyzed mostly at the level of I, SE, B and WO. However, there still exists a wide spectrum of human essences of life whose role is not completely explored in objective sciences. In such a situation, how can one expect the revelation of complete (or absolute) truth of Nature from the study of objective sciences? At this stage, it becomes necessary either to generalize the existing laws of objective sciences to accommodate the left-over or else to look for the new laws in the subjective science of which the existing laws of objective sciences turn out to be a special case. Patomic model only suggests a broad framework in this direction. Besides, the modelling process (whether it is done in religion or in science) also limits the complete understanding of a phenomenon in Nature.

Models could be descriptive or mathematical in nature. Now the question arises as to what extent the modelling and/or subsequent mathematization of the phenomenon can lead to the understanding of truth in absolute terms. Although a detailed answer to this question is already sought in Chap. 7, a few remarks can be made here. Since the assumptions are involved at every stage of development of a theory in science or a model in religion, the fact is that the understanding of the absolute truth remains highly limited. But this is how the science progresses. Perhaps the absolute truth remains a matter of realization only.

No doubt, the Vedānta philosophy is much deeper than ever conceived by the human mind. In this book, only some glimpses are given, which perhaps can offer a new line of thinking on the problems faced by the present day scientists in general, and physicists in particular for their basic or rather deeper understanding of these problems. It is only a matter of time when scientists will find so many verifications of the ideas already prevailing in Vedānta. After all the Lord Himself has said [80].

Vedeiśca sarveirahameva vedyo,
Vedānta kradvedavi dev cāhaṁ.

i.e. "It is I whom the four Vedas seek to know; nay, it is I who am the author of the Vedānta as well as the knower of the Vedas."

A one-line summary of the book can finally be put [81] in the words of Einstein as

"What does the fish know about water ? After all, it spends all its life in there."

Notes and References

1. Instead of philosophical atom type model we call in brief this model as 'patomic' model. While the first letter 'p' of the word philosophical is combined with the word atomic to make the word patomic, the dictionary meaning of this latter word can be derived from the word "patois" meaning thereby "differing materially from the literary language" which, in fact, speaks the correct spirit of the model proposed in Chap. 3 and is frequently used all throughout this book (see Sect. 3.5).

2. R.S. Kaushal, "Human Beings : From the Point of View of a Philosophical Atomic Model," Journ. Sc. and Ind. Res. (New Delhi) **49** (1990) 578 - 82.

3. See, for example, J.V. Narlikar, "*Introduction to Cosmology*" Cambridge Univ. Press, (First Indian Edition) 1993, p. 222.

4. See, for example, S. Mahadihassan, "The Five Elements of Chinese Cosmology in the Light of Dialecticism," Ind. Journ. Hist. Sc. **27**(1992) 1-3, and "A Comparative Study of Chinese Cosmology-cum-Humorology with Eight Elements," Ind. Journ. Hist. Sc. **24** (1989) 181-185.

5. See, for example, J.H. Gaisser and T.K. Gaisser, Ref. (26) and the Ref. (19) below.

6. Srīmad Bhagavad-Gītā, see, for example, Chap. 7, verse 4.

7. See, for example, Srīmadamritcandsurikṛit, "Tatwarthsar" ed. by Pt. Pannalal Sahityacarya (Sri Ganesh Prasad Varni Granthamala - 22 , Dumarabagh, Assi, Varanasi, 1970).

8. See, for example, J.C. Sikdar in "Study of Jainism" ed. by M.P. Marathe, M.A. Kelkar and P.P. Gokhale (I.P.Q. Publications, Pune, 1984), and J.C. Sikdar, "Fabric of Life : Paryapati Pranapan in Jain Agam," Ind. Journ. Hist. Sc. **27**(1992) 221-229. For a more recent survey on this subject see also, "*Tao of Jaina Sciences,* " (Arihant Publications, Dariba, Delhi, 1992).

9. Dr. Rudreshanand, "*Microvita : Cosmic Seeds of Life*" (Dharma Verlag, Weisenauer Weg 4, Mainz, Germany, 1988).

10. R.W. Sperry, "*Science and Moral Priority,* " New York, Columbia Univ. Press, 1983.

11. David Hastenes, "Modelling Games in Newtonian World," Am. J. Phys. **60** (1992) 732-48.

12. Amit Goswami, "Consciousness in Quantum Physics and the Mind-Body Problem," Journ. of Mind and Behaviour **11** (1990) 75-96, and the reference therein.

13. K. Popper and J. Eccles, "The Self and Its Brain" (Springer Verlag, Berlin 1981), as cited in Ref. (11).

14. Srīmad Bhagavad-Gītā, Chap. 3, Verse 42.

15. E.P. Wigner in, I.J. Good (Ed.), "*The Scientist Speculates*", Kindswood, Surrey, England, The Windmill Press (1962).

16. Srīmad Bhagavad-Gītā, Chap. 3, Verse 27.

17. This fact, often quoted in the Hindu philosophy is supported by "Sa hi vaiṣnavo yad vāmanāḥ; Vāmano has viṣnurāsā," Satpath Brahmana, 5.2.5.4. and 1.2.5.5, respectively.

18. Though, to a good deal of accuracy the validity of this law is already known in the case of electromagnetic interactions between elementary particles, the validity is also noticed in recent times at the level of quark model for strong interactions : see for example, T. Appelquist and H.D. Politzer. Phys Rev. Lett. **34** (1975) **43** : R.S. Kaushal & D.S. Kulshreshtha. Ann. Phys. (N.Y.). **108** (1977), 198.

19. David Harrison, Am. J. Phys. 46 (1978) 432.

20. Srīmad Bhagawad-Gītā, Chap. 7, Verse 4.

21. As far as the ordering of mind, intellect, ego and soul is concerned it is further supported by another verse (Chap. 3, verse 42) of Srīmad Bhagawad-Gītā. The Samkhya philosophy, however, maintains another eight-fold mode of nature, namely, Pradhān, Mahattatva, Ego and five Tanmātrās. Here, however, we shall adopt the eight-fold (insentient) mode of nature as described in the Gītā.

22. A.S. Eddington, "*The Philosophy of Physical Sciences*" (Cambridge Univ. Press, 1939), p. 7.

23. R.S. Kaushal, "Laws of Physical Sciences and the Human Behaviour." (Spiritual India and Kundalini, Delhi-6) Vol. *II* (1978), p.17.

24. A.S. Eddington, "*The Philosophy of Physical Sciences,*" p. 22.

25. M. Gell-Mann, Phys, Lett. **8** (1964) 214 : J.J.J. Kokkedee "*The Quark Model*" (New York, Benjamin, 1969) and the references therein: A.N. Mitra and R. Majumdar, Phys. Rev. **150** (1966) 1194.

26. Julia H. Gaisser and T.K. Gaisser, Am. J. Phys. **45** (1977) 439.

27. H. Harari, Phys. Lett. **86B** (1979) 83 : M.A. Shupe Phys. Lett. **86B** (1979) 87 : A.N. Mitra, Phys. Rev. **D28** (1983) 1745.

28. J.G. Taylor, "Can Neural Networks ever be Made to Think," Neural Network World 1 (1991) 1-3;' Proc. of Second Int. Wigmer Symp., Goslar (FRG), July 15-20 1991; Private communications.

29. For a nice review on this subject see, for example, Amit Goswami, "Idealistic Interpretations of Quantum Mechanics," Phys. Essays **2** (1989) 385-400; Amit Goswami, "*Quantum Mechanics*" (Wm. C. Brown Publishers, 1992), p. 517.

30. See, Refs. (12) and (13).

31. See, for example, A. Salam and J. Strathadee, Ann. Phys. (NY) 141 (1982) 316.

32. Paramhans Yogānanda, "*Vākya Sudhā*" (Belan Ganj, Agra).

33. Similar meaning can be understood for other senses of knoweldge vis-a-vis the corresponding sense objects.

34. See, for example, Ishwar Krishna, "Sāṁkhyakārikā," Eng. Translation with notes by S.S. Surya Narayan Sastri, (Adyar Library Pub., Madras, 1973).

35. It may be mentioned that in recent years there has been considerable progress in the understanding of these four fundamental interactions of physics. While mediators responsible for these interactions (namely, gluon for strong, photon for electromagnetic, W-boson for weak and graviton for gravitational interaction) are now more or less established, the possibility of their common origin (unification) at very high laboratory energies is also noticed wihin a common mathematical framework. However, the limitations (in terms of the mathematical complexity and the validity of standard physical laws) on the underlying mathematical modelling do not allow the experts to think anything subtle beyond these fields of physics. For example, while the nonlinearity of the underlying field equations in supergravity and/or string field theories of physics poses one type of problem, the principle of causality, on the other hand, is taken as a God-given reality.

36. A.A. Michelson and H.G. Gale, "The Effect of the Earth's rotation on the velocity of light" Astrophys. J. 61 (1925) 140, as cited in "Pseudo-Relativistic Physics" by Antonis Agathangelidis (1991).

37. Iśāvāsyopaniṣad (Shankarbhasya), Chap. 6, p. 25, Verse 4.

38. We call this nonphysical matter as epiphysical in the spirit of the meaning of the prefix "epi." The dictionary meaning of this prefix is "on the ground of" or "in addition" to

physical which carries the correct sprit of the ideas under discussion.

39. G.L. Pandit, "Methodological Variance; Essays in Epistemological Ontology and Methodology of Science" in Boston Studies in the Philosophy of Science, Vol. 131, 1991.

40. See, for example, Ref. (29); A. Aspect; Phys. Lett. **54A** (1975) 117; E.P. Wigner, "*Symmetries and Reflections*" (Indiana Univ. Press, 1967).

41. For the description of Twin Paradox, see, for example, D. Kleppner and R.J. Kolenkow, "*An Introduction to Mechanics*" (McGraw Hill Book Co., 1973), p. 480.

42. S.M. Roy, "The EPR Paradox" Phys. News **11** (1980) 1 and the references therein.

43. J. Von Neumann, "*Mathematical Foundations of Quantum Mechanics,* " Princeton, New Jersey, Princeton Univ. Press, 1955.

44. See, for example, B. Eckhardt, Phys. Rep. **163** (1988) 206, R.S. Kaushal, Ann. Phys. (NY) **206** (1991) 90.

45. David Bohm, "*Quantum Theory*" (Prentice Hall, Englewood Cliffs, New Jersey, 1951); For a recent review see, for example, D. Bohm, B.J. Hiley, and P.N. Kaloyerou, Phys. Rep. **144** (1987) 323.

46. C.W. Misner and J.A. Wheeler, "Classical Physics as Geometry," Ann. Phys. (NY) **2** (1957) 525 (footnote no. 9a); E. Schrodinger, "*My View of the World*" translated by C. Hastings (Cambridge Univ. Press, 1964), p. 18.

47. See Ref. (19).

48. Īśāvāsyopaniṣad (Shankara Bhaṣya), opening and concluding verses.

49. See, for example, "*Vivek Cūdāmani*" —Srī Adyaśnkarācārya Viracit, Verses, 89, 98, 122.

50. It may be remarked that lately scientists have also realized the non-existence of life on several other planets of our solar system. In fact, the conditions in the sense of mahābhūtās may not prevail there to give rise to the full $\mathscr{G}$-form for the manifestation of SO. However, since $\mathscr{M}$ is also partly affected by the presence of mahābhūtas, $\mathscr{C} \cup \mathscr{M}$ in its deformed form, can very well exist there.

51. Note that these five tanmātrās τ_{ea}, τ_{w}, τ_{a}, τ_{f} and τ_{et} correspondingly represent the quanta of interaction of the human being with pañca mahābhūtās: earth, water, air, fire and ether as described in Chap. 4 and they are labelled accordingly. Here, in this Section, however we ignore the effect of these tanmātrās on each human being for the sake of simplicity.

52. For a review on this subject see, Ref. (29).

53. See, for example, Srīmad Bhagvad-Gītā, Chap. 6, Verse 35,36; Chap. 2, Verses 55-72.

54. See, for example, Srīmad Bhagavad-Gītā, Chap. 2, Verses 55-72.

55. See, for example Ref. (49), and Srīmad Bhagavad-Gītā Chap. 18.

56. *"Vivek-Cūdāmani"* Srī-Ādyaṣankarācārya Viracit, verse 174.

57. In spite of the fact that WO could be the same, it may appear to be different for the different beings depending upon the mental set-up or on the degree of relative consciousness of each human being.

58. For a recent work, see, for example, special issue on "Mathematical Modelling of Innovation, Diffusion and Technological Changes" ed. by Karmeshu, Journ. Sc. and Ind. Res. 51 (1992) no. 3; Also, see no. 8, a special issue on "Mathematical Modelling of Science and Technology Studies."

59. V. Mahajan and R.A. Peterson, *"Models for Innovation Diffusion"* (Sage Publication, Beverly Hills, CA, 1985).

60. See, for example, "Religion in an Age of Science" by Ian Barbour, as reviewed by E.E. Selk in Am. J. Phys. **59** (1991) 1152-53.

61. See, for example, "*Mathematical Models in Biology and Medicine*" by J.N. Kapoor (Affiliated East-West Press, N. Delhi, 1985).

62. D.J. Bartholomew, "*Stochastic Models for Social Processes,*" (John Wiley, New York, 1982).

63. W. Weidlich and G. Haag. "*Concepts and Models of a Quantitative Sociology : The Dynamics of Interacting Populations*" (Springer Verlag, Berlin, 1983).

64. G. Holton, "*Thematic Origins of Scientific Thought,*" Harvard Univ. Press, 1973.

65. In fact data (or observations) in science can vary over a wide range i.e. from the level of thought—experiment down to the level of actual laboratory experiment. Accordingly, within the framework of certain laws or postulates (which are again deduced or extracted generally from another set of data) the models have to describe the observed reality (nature) but the models for the thought - experiments are crucial (in the sense of revolutionizing the whole discipline), somewhat longer lived whereas those for the laboratory experiments are phenomenological. For details see Sects. 7.4 and 7.5.

66. Srīmad Bhagawad-Gītā, Chap. 18.

67. S.M. Roy, "The EPR Paradox" Phys. News **11** (1980) 1, and the references therein; Amit Goswami, "Idealistic Interpretations of Quantum Mechanics," Phys. Essays **2** (1989) 385-400.

68. A.R. Verma, Private Communications.

69. Srīmad Bhagawad-Gītā, Chap. 2, see, for example, verses 17-20.

70. Iśāvāsyopaniṣad (Shankara Bhasya) verse 5.

71. See, for example, Ref. (11).

72. Some of these phenomena are cited in, R.S. Kaushal, Ann. Phys, (NY) **206** (1991) 90-105.

73. A.N. Mitra, "Parameters of Physics Perspectives : Principle, Postulates and Prejudices," Phys. News 21 (1990) 7.

74. See, for example, A. Salam and J. Strathadee, Ann. Phys. (NY) 141 (1982) 316.

75. Johathan Swift, "A Thought for Today" Times of India, Sept. 4, 1993.

76. See, for example, Śvetāṣvatara Upaniṣad and Refs. (7), (32) and (34) above.

77. J.D. Bjorken and S.D. Drell, "*Relativistic Quantum Fields*" McGraw-Hill Book Co., 1965, p. 17 ; L.D. Landau and E.M. Lifshitz, "*Classical Theory of Fields,*" Perganon Press, 1975.

78. Srīmad Bhagavad-Gītā, see chapters 3 and 5.

79. Swami Jitatmanand, "*Modern Physics and Vedānta,*" Bharatiya Vidya Bhavan Publication, 1992.

80. Srīmad Bhagavad-Gītā, Chap. 15, Verse 15.

81. Albert Einstein, "The World as I See It" (1935).

Index